HIRE ME, INC.

INTERVIEWS

That Get Offers

HIRE ME, INC.
INTERVIEWS

That Get Offers

ROY J.
BLITZER

EP
Entrepreneur
Press

Editorial director: Jere L. Calmes
Cover design: Beth Hansen-Winter
Composition and production: Eliot House Productions

This publication is designed to provide accurate and authoritative information in regard to the subject matter covered. It is sold with the understanding that the publisher is not engaged in rendering legal, accounting, or other professional services. If legal advice or other expert assistance is required, the services of a competent professional person should be sought.

Library of Congress Cataloging-in-Publication Data
    Blitzer, Roy J.
    Hire me, Inc.: interviews that get offers/by Roy J. Blitzer.
       p.   cm.
     ISBN 1-59918-038-3 (alk. paper)
     1. Employment interviewing. I. Title.
    HF5549.5.I6B472 2006
    650.14'4—dc22   2006026785

Printed in Canada

11 10 09 08 07 06   10 9 8 7 6 5 4 3 2 1

CONTENTS

CHAPTER 3

MORE COMPETENCIES
What Else Is Your Employer Looking For? _____ **43**

CHAPTER 4

TECHNICAL AND
BEHAVIORAL OPTIONS _____ **75**

ACKNOWLEDGMENTS

Anyone in the creative arts will verify that it takes much more than an hour and often more than 60 people to produce CBS's *60 Minutes*. Certainly creating this book cannot be compared to an Emmy award-winning news show, but a great many people and lots of their time and energy helped make this text a reality.

I'd first like to thank my colleagues in the career counseling profession—friends and co-workers who worked side-by-side with me providing career counseling and outplacement services through the years—first at Syntex Corporation (now Roche Pharmaceuticals-F. Hoffman-LaRocheLtd.), then at de Recat/Interim/Spherion, and now at TMS, Torchiana, Mastrov and Sapiro. (Especially Al, Anna, Anne, Beth, Bert, Bill, Cathy, Cheryl, Connie, Dave, Enid, Eve, Gary, Gene, Helen, Holly, Jack, Janet, Kathy, Kristi, Laura, Lido, Margot, Marlys, Maryann, Mary, Maureen, Megan, Mike, Pat, Steve, Sue, Susan, and Susie.) You have been unselfish in sharing your experiences, previously created notes and written manuals/materials, and what-works tips of the trade. All have been lovingly massaged and painstakingly altered and as part of the content of this book will now continue to help a whole new set of people. I am forever grateful and appreciative to you and your professionalism.

Special appreciation to my agent, Jeff Herman, and the Jeff Herman Literary Agency. His support and faith in my skills has been extraordinary and responsible for this project series.

Kudos also to Jim Hennessy and Jacquie Reynolds Rush, who read the early chapter drafts and contributed special insight and important data to make them better.

All of the staff at Entrepreneur Media, my editor Karen Thomas in particular, and Karen Billipp and Jere Calmes in the background, deserve recognition for their patience and understanding, especially of my limited but constantly improving word processing and computer skills.

Finally, thanks to my immediate family. To my wife Carol, a seasoned journalist and the legitimate writer in our group, for her support—and huge chunks of time—in final writing, proofing, and editing. To our daughters, Mara and Hannah, for their willingness to practice some of these interviewing skills and for getting results that launched their professional lives so successfully and admirably.

PREFACE

Talk to anybody about his or her experience of getting a job and the interview is *always* mentioned. Stories abound, both positive and horrible, about the job interview, and nearly everyone has an opinion on what to do and what not to do. The job interview is perhaps the most vital part of your job search. Just like the salesperson must prospect and qualify before (s)he makes the pitch, so must you. Indeed, there is more to getting a job than getting the interview, though in many ways that call to present yourself to an interested future employer is the first significant accomplishment and reward of your search/career process. Take a bow. Enjoy it. Just be aware that how you perform at this critical event is the real test, and the offer of employment the ultimate goal.

The aim of *Hire Me, Inc.: Interviews that Get Offers* is to prepare you for this experience. The positive result is being called back to continue the interview process or to be in the offer process. It helps you present yourself as a special talent in the marketplace so you become the desired product in the employment arena. You are about to launch this one-of-a-kind resource, and the interview is your most important sales presentation, the "pitch" you make to the customer that will make you a "must have" and close the deal.

The mantra in the world of real estate is location, location, location; the mantra for getting a job or finding the perfect career (see my book *Hire Me, Inc.*) is networking, networking, networking. Here, the mantra for a successful interview is "preparation, preparation, preparation."

Throughout the text you'll be provided lots of opportunities to experiment and to look at practice options. It is important to practice hearing your answers. The more comfortable you are with your responses, the more easily your answers will flow in real time. Video practice helps with your "look," and audio and in person practice increases your comfort level. You'll also find some handy Practical Tips and Opinions (PTOs) that appear in each section and provide either summarized or additional tips for your enrichment. Here's an example:

PTOS (Practical Tips and Opinions)

Personal sales is still the most important ingredient of Promotion—the fourth "P" of your marketing mix that also includes Product, Price, and Place.

- Knowing yourself and assessing your strengths and improvement areas are the first steps to effective sales presentations.

- Treat every interview as the most important one. There is no casual, just shoot-the-breeze discussion. You are always being evaluated.

> ## PTOS   (Practical Tips and Opinions)
>
> • Be alert. Listen carefully to what your interviewer is really asking and watch closely for signals of what (s)he is really doing or telegraphing (nervous fiddling, facial expressions, body language, etc.). These interview observations and assessments need to be integrated into your presentation and will help improve the quality of both your answers and questions.

There are also HITs—Hints, Insights, and Thoughts—sidebars interspersed throughout each chapter to provide additional points of interest or special tidbits that can help make a difference in your success.

So . . . pick yourself up, dust yourself off, find your favorite interview outfit, and start to prepare for this exciting experience. You will probably learn as much about yourself or those who will try to get to know you by interviewing you for a job or a new career adventure. Take advantage of this learning and enjoy the process.

Dedication

This book is dedicated to those people whom I may have helped in some way to discover their passion and to earn their livelihoods in jobs and careers they love.

My hope is that they will bring inspiration to those still searching, and the future workplace will be filled with happy and productive individuals. The journey for job/career satisfaction is well worth the effort—your joy at doing what you're good at, what you love, and what's important to you can make that long-term difference.

MARKET ANALYSIS

The Boy Scouts of America (and perhaps the Girl Scouts now, as well) have had the right idea all along: **Be prepared**. Your sales presentation will be a winner if you do as much preparation as you can—about yourself, about the company, about the position, and about the people who will be interviewing you.

DOING YOUR HOMEWORK

This entire text is really a preparation assignment. Both the content of what you say—your answer—and your process—how you look and how you say it—need to be polished for the interview to be a success. You must know who you are and how to present yourself to be consistent and congruent.

For now, let's take a big picture view and start with you. (In later chapters, you will dig deeper into what and how to prepare.) What are you good at? What *qualities* have been singled out as your strengths? Where do you get your compliments? See Figure 1.1.

Then look to how you could be better. What are some areas where you want to improve or have been told you need some help? What skill requires additional mastery or where do you falter and make mistakes? (Areas to

Figure 1.1: **Your Strengths**

List at least five areas where you shine. (Refer to past performance evaluations, letters of recommendation, or even old report cards. How would a close friend or relative describe your best skills and abilities?)

Consider these to be your product features, the things you do best and make you special.

Strengths

1. _____

2. _____

3. _____

4. _____

5. _____

Figure 1.2: **Your Weaknesses**

Provide five improvement points.

Areas of Improvement (Weaknesses)

1. _____

2. _____

3. _____

4. _____

5. _____

improve are also part of a good performance evaluation and review discussion.) See Figure 1.2.

Another way to gain greater personal insight is to take a personality assessment. The most well documented and researched tool in the United States today is the Myers Briggs Type Indicator (MBTI). Based on the work done by psychologist Carl Jung, it measures, in a nonjudgmental way, your preferences on four dimensions: Where you get your energy (*Extravert vs. Introvert*); What you pay attention to (*Sensing vs. Intuitive*); How you make decisions (*Thinking vs. Feeling*); and How you live your life (*Perceiving vs. Judging*). Understanding the results can help you do everything from communicating more effectively and making better decisions to solving problems more easily, working more collaboratively in teams, and managing conflict less stressfully.

All personality preference types share hallmark characteristics that can help provide you with a better understanding of how each individual communicates, comprehends, and makes judgments about information and experience in his/her own unique manner. With knowledge of personality types, you will soon

HITS (Hints, Insights, and Thoughts)

Remember, there *is no new feedback*. As we go through life, we get lots of input (and advice) and much of it, unfortunately, is critical. If you are totally honest with yourself, coming up with five areas to work on should not be that difficult. Again, think of someone who really cares about you. What would (s)he say were your weaknesses? What have you been consistently hearing over the years?

Also remember, every strength done in excess becomes a liability. The warm, talkative, outgoing, life-of-the-party guy can be the same person who takes up too much airtime in a meeting or finishes someone's incomplete thoughts or interrupts a slow talker.

be able to look for clues that indicate how closely you are meeting the needs of your interviewer.

Most career centers will administer the MBTI and provide a certified professional to interpret the results for you. Should you choose to work with a career counselor/consultant, (s)he might also use the assessment as a way to get to know you and to search for career options that suit your style. You can also take the instrument for free on the internet (www.humanmetrics.com/cgi-win/Jtypes2.asp), but the interpretation and application pieces are especially lightweight.

Later in the chapter you will prepare your product benefits, a list of accomplishments that will help the interviewer see what you can do to solve a key problem or bring extra value to the organization. Now, put some thought into your package—how you look.

How you present yourself—your "look"—is another key ingredient in your sales presentation/promotion process. You need to be sure to put some preparation into this element. Get a good night's rest. Look fresh, rested, and fit. (Maybe this is a good time to be toning up and shedding those extra pounds.)

Be photo ready at all times. Keep your hair and nails clean and in good shape. Be sure you have at least two interview outfits that fit properly and are ready to go (in case you are called in on short notice or are asked back the next day or the same week). Each needs to be comfortable (for what could be six to eight hours of interviewing) and accessorized appropriately. More details and particulars on your product *package* (dress and overall appearance) will be covered in Chapter 5, but it's best in the first interview, even in the most casual of environments, for men to wear a tie and jacket and for women to wear a businesslike suit. Your goal in this customer research/preparation, do-your-homework phase is to know your audience and to telegraph that you not only can fit but can also clean up well and put your most professional foot forward.

LISTING YOUR ACCOMPLISHMENTS

Perhaps your final personal preparation comes in how you describe and present your accomplishments. If your strengths (and areas of improvement) are your *product features*, the qualities *you have*, then your accomplishments are your *benefits*, what *you can do* for the organization and how you can transfer your previous successes to bring added value.

> **HITS** (Hints, Insights, and Thoughts)
>
> There are many assessment instruments on the market in addition to the MBTI that can bring personal insight. The Strong Inventory provides job categories related to interests. THE BIRKMAN provides, among other data points, information on stress behaviors. The DISC provides personality data, and the FIRO-B focuses on control issues. You will benefit tremendously by completing some kind of assessment instrument.

You need to reflect back to your previous experiences and look to your resume. Imagine the exercise like making an OAR (opportunity, action, result), a necessary tool that will help you row to the finish line.

1. *What was the **O**pportunity (or problem) you were presented?* These examples can come from a former work assignment, a volunteer project, or any relevant event where you actively participated. Be sure to include, if you can, all names, places, and numbers so the interviewer will be able to see future applications.

2. *What **A**ction did you take or what **A**ctivity did you sponsor?* Did you remove a roadblock or eliminate a conflict or create a new process? (Use "I" here vs. the royal "we." Being a team player is important, but the interviewer is hiring you now, not the team.)

3. *What was the **R**esult?* What was accomplished? What did you learn? How did your group benefit? Again, be specific and provide as much metric data as you can: 30 percent increase in sales; 20 percent decrease in shipping mistakes; 4.5 out of 5 satisfaction rating.

With your resume as the primary reference point, use the worksheet in Figure 1.3 to highlight your benefits, single out your accomplishments, and capture your success stories.

Figure 1.3: **Your Accomplishments**

Remember what OAR stands for and fill in your top four professional achievements.

O pportunity or problem that existed—what were your responsibilities?

A ctivity—what did you *do* to identify the issue or resolve the problem?

R esults—what did you accomplish? What were the metrics in your success?

Accomplishment 1

O _____

_____

A _____

_____

R _____

_____

Accomplishment 2

O _____

_____

A _____

_____

R _____

_____

Accomplishment 3

O _____

_____

A _____

_____

Figure 1.3: **Your Accomplishments,** continued

R _____

_____

Accomplishment 4

O _____

_____

A _____

_____

R _____

_____

My key marketable skills are: _____

_____

_____

_____

My distinction from other candidates is: _____

_____

_____

_____

My unique value to the organization is: _____

_____

_____

_____

You must be ready to explain your success stories succinctly and to present those measurable achievements and results as not only benefiting your organization but also meeting and/or exceeding the requirements of your job.

Another preparation point is learning as much as you can about the company. Here you can turn to the internet as an invaluable source. Spend some time on the organization's web site. Ferret out as much data as possible about the vision, the management, the products, the market, and the competition. What is the site telling you? Has lots of marketing money been invested into high-tech bells and whistles? Is it easy or complex to navigate? How much real data is provided, and how much is implied or left to the imagination? What is the mix of the senior management team? Have they all gone to the same university or worked for the same organization? If there are pictures included, can you draw any conclusions from them?

Get the most recent annual report. Check the financials. If necessary, work with an accounting or finance friend to get help interpreting or understanding anything. Dig again here for product competitive market and personnel data.

Brochures, especially product pieces such as spec sheets, advertisements, etc., also present a picture of the organization that you might be able to use in your answers (and questions) and as points to consider when making your decision to accept an offer. Your local library may have what you want, but you can certainly call the promotion department to send you the literature that will help increase your overall knowledge.

Often the most powerful source of company information and the most reliable data come from people who work there. You might learn something about the environment or culture, or pick up some tips about the hiring manager, the corporate management style, or the job itself. Be sure you know the exact spelling and pronunciation of each person's name, especially the hiring manager. (If you're in doubt, the receptionist will usually clarify names for you.)

Now is a chance to tap your network. Ask around. Pick a brain or two. Send an e-mail call for help. Who knows an employee who works there? How can (s)he help you make contact to collect some data? Perhaps the person who introduced you to this opportunity is enough.

When/if you make any inside connection, be sure to ask questions with answers that are difficult to obtain through other, more public sources. Questions with information show the interviewer that you did indeed do your homework and are fully prepared for the time (s)he was giving you. Some of this information you can ask in the interview—from your hiring manager, from HR, or from future peers. Other kinds you may be able to get from a search firm or company recruiter. But knowing the inside skinny beforehand can only help distinguish you.

Some areas where information can be vital include:

- *The company and its business*
  - How is the company reacting to *X trend* (maybe outsourcing)?
  - What has the organization done to strengthen itself against the prevailing economic downturn? How does it feel about layoffs vs. other measures (salary reductions, reduced work week, unpaid time off, etc.)?
  - What are the driving factors that protect market share?

- *The product*
  - What are the key reasons the main product is returned? Why does it fail?
  - What is the key competitor's pitch to encourage an existing customer to switch?
  - How many new products are in the pipeline?

- *Your future boss*
  - What is my hiring manager's reputation? How is (s)he referenced?

HITS (Hints, Insights, and Thoughts)

Be careful what you wish for. All too often honest answers to these kinds of questions may give you information that puts up lots of red flags and points to a position you might not really want. To calibrate what could be a personal bias, try to talk to more than one person or at least to someone like you or who might share your approach to work. At this pre-interview, homework stage, remain open and receptive to finding out for yourself and for waiting until you have an offer in hand (and everything else you need) to pass critical judgment and to make an informed yes or no decision. Your reaction to what you hear, if it is not enthusiastic and very interested, should not be telegraphed in the interview.

- How do new employees get feedback? Long-standing employees?
- What kind of person does (s)he work with best?

- *The environment/culture*
  - How do people have fun here? Handle difficult times?
  - What did the staff who interviewed me do to sell or overtly encourage me to take the job? And how did that compare to the way you were treated the first day and few weeks?
  - Why do most people leave the organization? (How were they treated on departure?)

- *The position*
  - Why is the position open? New requisition or replacement?
  - How often are the bonuses in this job distributed? What happens when you don't meet targets and still work yourself to the bone?
  - What is the reporting structure?

- *Your competition*
  - What are the profiles of the other people being considered?
  - Is there an internal candidate in consideration?
  - What order will I be "presented"?

If possible, visit the company's location. You can test the drive time, check out the office ambiance and work tempo, and see how employees dress as well. Although it's not quite the research for landing on the Moon, you can never have too much information for landing a job.

USING THE JOB DESCRIPTION

Now is the time to study and prepare for the job itself. The best way to begin is to create a *T cover letter* (also called an *echo cover letter*) for the position you will be interviewing. Use the advertisement, job posting, or listing to generate a sheet with a direct comparison between the job requirements and your qualifications. Look at the example for sample letters before trying your own in Figure 1.4. It's a visual match (although in some cases just a partial one) between what the job needs and how you can fulfill it, and can be put to memory for a sales-positioning interview or left at the close of your meeting as a reminder of your suitability and fit.

Sample #1
WAREHOUSE SUPERVISOR

Customized food distribution corporation looking for a full-time Warehouse Supervisor. Excellent salary and benefits package provided. Applicant must be a self-starter, leader, willing to work night shift, and have three years' relevant experience. Degree preferred but not required. #505056

YOUR REQUIREMENTS	MY BACKGROUND
Self-starter	Designed and implemented two warehouse programs
Leadership ability	Managed crew of four with 0 percent turnover
Willing to work night shift	Led night shift staff four years (prefer those hours)
Three years relevant experience	Four years in industry
Degree preferred but not required	BS Operations Management

Sample #2
HUMAN RESOURCE PERSONNEL OFFICER

We are a large real estate brokerage looking for a Human Resource Personnel Officer with seven-plus years' experience in recruiting and hiring industry professionals. Must be familiar with the business, have administrative experience, and the ability to work collaboratively under pressure. BA/BS required. Reference #23465.

YOUR REQUIREMENTS	MY BACKGROUND
Recruiting and hiring	Attracted and retained key talent with a turnover rate 50 percent below industry average
Direct administrative activities	Assisted manager in planning and executing all company HR programs
Real estate industry knowledge	CA real estate agent license
Seven years' experience	Eight years at G & G—three years as an agent
BA/BS required	BS Business Management

Figure 1.4: **T Cover Letter Worksheet**

Your requirements for the SENIOR SALES REPRESENTATIVE match my qualifications as follows:

YOUR REQUIREMENTS   **MY QUALIFICATIONS**

_____   _____

_____   _____

_____   _____

_____   _____

_____   _____

Sometimes, when competition is especially fierce or for certain professional positions—bench scientists, product marketing managers, stand-up trainers, librarians, and especially a children's librarian—you may be required to deliver a group presentation or mini-seminar as part of the interview process. Customer research here is also important, particularly in finding out as early in the process as you can when this would take place. (Typically, it is after a successful set of interviews and used as another assessment tool for the final decision.)

Try to do as much pre-work as you can and have the shell of generic presentation ready to go—PowerPoint™, hand-outs, etc. You should be alert and energetic, not exhausted from a last-minute all-nighter at your computer.

Generating Possible Questions

Your goal for this kind of pre-interview preparation should be a no-surprise experience. Try to figure out what questions you will encounter. Put yourself in the shoes of the interviewer and create a set of questions that you would want to ask. For those of you who have had years of hiring experience, this might not be too much of a stretch.

What *qualities* are unique to the individual performing tasks in this position? What kind of person is needed to be successful? Look to the job description again, of course. It might be stated there already. What are the other team managers or executives looking for? What are the requirements, and how will (s)he get the information needed?

Prepare answers that positively illustrate your OAR stories, answers that will help to position your personal benefits and features to match exactly what will help the organization most, and eventually make the hiring manager look like a hero/heroine for selecting the best resource possible. Read the following examples of OAR stories and then use the worksheet in Figure 1.5.

> **HITS** (Hints, Insights, and Thoughts)
>
> Good presentations are like good interviews. The same sales and promotion skills apply. Practicing the tips below should help:
> - Prepare a clear objective of what you want
> - Stimulate interest
> - Present your key point
> - Provide supporting data
> - Close with a summary and action recommendation
>
> Tailoring your delivery as much as possible will also help connect with your audience—using the same or similar company color for your slide background or referencing their product, etc. Remember also not to wear your Omega watch if you are presenting to a team that produces Movados.

Sample preparation question sheet:

Quality	Possible Question
Good Customer Service Skills	"Tell me about the toughest customer you had and what you did to win him/her to your side."

OAR Story Answer

I was hoping that I'd get a chance to talk about H.B. I inherited an influential and large customer account that consistently had mistakes in both its shipping and billing, and the client was constantly badgering the staff to fix these fast.

The customer was ready to take his business elsewhere, too. I researched the problems, then drove three hours to the company's location for a personal meeting and explained the causes of the errors. I made time-based commitments for improvement and positive change on our side with the condition that he would pledge to treat our staff cordially on his requests.

The volume of his business increased 25 percent over the next three months, and our mistakes and his behavior improved substantially. I was seen as a sort of miracle worker after that solution—and when the customer moved on to another company, he even renewed his business with us.

Quality	Possible Question
Ability to multitask	"What is a busy day for you? How do you handle it and how do you know you were successful?"

OAR Story Answer

I'm pleased you inquired. Jumble's reception desk was always a bevy of activity, even on so-called quiet days. One Tuesday morning from about 8:00 to 10:30, I greeted and signed in the recruits from around the world visiting us for sales training—badges, packets, etc.—distributed the mail into our boxes, answered and transfered all incoming calls, including occasional pages, and checked in the string of FedEx and UPS morning deliveries. I just kept my composure, smiled and chuckled a lot, and knew all had gone well when a visiting consultant waiting in the lobby to coach our CEO passed on a compliment on my lack of mistakes and unflappable style. He even told the CEO, and last October, I won the Employee of the Month award!

Quality	Possible Question
Team Player—Collaborative	"How do you define a team player? Provide a personal example that illustrates your definition."

OAR Story Answer

There are probably lots of acceptable definitions here, but since you asked, a team player is someone who knows his/her role and the responsibility that goes with it. In my world, a team player is someone able to see beyond his/her personal gain for the success of the team and/or task at hand.

At CCC we rotated our presentation responsibilities, and I was next in the cue to present our creative campaign to a relatively new but potentially big-spending client. I agreed to break order and give up that opportunity when we learned that another artist on our team went to grad school with the new client. All of us were confident that the client relationship would be solidified and made much stronger with a more familiar face at the PowerPoint.

This was not easy, to say the least. I had not made a presentation in a while, and it was a favorite part my job. All worked out, that client spent a fortune, and my next presentation yielded the biggest print campaign spending in the agency's history—about $5,000 per month.

Figure 1.5: **Question Preparation Worksheet**

Quality   **Possible Question**

_____   _____

OAR Story Answer

_____

_____

_____

Quality   **Possible Question**

_____   _____

OAR Story Answer

_____

_____

_____

Quality   **Possible Question**

_____   _____

OAR Story Answer

_____

_____

_____

PTOS (Practical Tips and Opinions)

- The information that will help you most about the company and the people who will interview you will come from someone inside the organization. Press for straight talk and honest input (no party line or B.S.), and then be prepared to filter it.

- At minimum, know the company's stock price, key competitors, and latest public policies or issues. (You might also learn the credentials of those interviewing you. You might discover a network peer.)

- In your dry-run visit, plan to spend a few moments in the parking lot or think of a reason to get to the cafeteria. You will benefit from getting a look at the site and seeing what the staff looks like and wears.

- It's best not to have your first contact/job interview at a restaurant or bar. Eating or drinking can distract both of you and can compete for attention needed for the data-gathering and assessment process.

- Lean on a trusted friend or relative to provide you feedback. Choose someone who won't hesitate to pass on everything from an alternative route and/or shortcut to your interview site—and maybe avoiding a traffic bottleneck—to honest input on the two outfits and accessories you selected to wear.

- Knowing your customer and doing the research *is* important, but the salespeople who find ways to integrate the information into the dialogue or weave the data into a well-crafted answer or artful question usually get the sale. You must use your research as well as know it.

The final part of your customer research at this stage is related to *Place* in your marketing mix. Know exactly where you will have your interview and after securing accurate directions, do a dry run. Test how long it takes to get there with traffic and without. Remember: *Never be late for an interview*. There are no valid excuses, especially for the first visit. Press to meet at the office so you can assess the environment and check out the staff (Dress all alike? Young and hip? Older?).

✳ *Summary* ✳

✳ Knowing yourself—refocusing on your features (strengths and areas of improvement) and benefits (measurable accomplishments and results)—is the first step to doing solid customer research.

✳ Doing your homework should be a dig-deep process of gathering as much relevant data as you can about the company, its product or service, the position, the direct manager, and the competition. Reading and observation are valuable and necessary but, if possible, need to be supplemented by asking key questions and talking directly to someone who has first-hand exposure and is well meaning and direct.

✳ Preparing is ongoing and constant, yet at this stage should include everything from having your clothing and personal presence "ready to go" to driving to the interview site beforehand to check out the staff, surroundings, time, and difficulty.

COMPETENCIES
What Are Employers Really Looking For?

Fit, chemistry, match. These are words that are often used when employers are searching for top talent and want to hire the best individual possible. You can increase the odds of fitting in, generating the right chemistry, and creating a solid match if you know in advance what kind of person your employer is looking for and can provide the appropriate and relevant answers that satisfy the criteria.

Although each organization sees itself as unique, many organizations in today's fast-paced and ever-changing work environments manage to a set of competencies: a series of qualities that they want their employees and managers to have. These are generic, tradition-proven skills that when in place increase performance success. In preparing for your interview, look to the competencies listed here and in Chapter 3, the possible questions that could be asked, and the evaluation possibilities as another way to get ready. Study each sample and then fill out Figure 2.1. Your goal is to sell and position your competencies to the organization.

ANALYTICAL SKILL

Possible Questions

What stumbling blocks have you had to overcome in the past? How did you get around them?

Evaluation

Does the candidate recognize barriers? Or, is (s)he a "coyote" in a roadrunner scenario?

OAR Story Answer

I'll go back to my recent academic experience for this one because that's fresh in my mind. My thesis advisor, mentor, and key champion was taken ill two days before I defended my dissertation, and I was leaving right afterwards for a series of out-of-town job interviews—all for positions that were dependent on my "passing" and receiving the degree. This was not an easy fix because no one really knew how long she would be in recovery. I needed her there no matter what, so I scrambled and arranged for a new date (with assurances that the rest of my committee would be present, as well) a few months out and came clean about my situation, taking a straight approach with everyone interested in hiring me. National came up with a super offer and must have appreciated my honesty. My advisor, fortunately, was back in five weeks. I flew back on company time and presented successfully enough to get my degree. That National position, it turned out, led to the initial DDI research and my first patent.

Figure 2.1: **Analytical Skill Worksheet**

Possible Questions

Everyone blows one on occasion. Describe your last major goof. Why did it happen? What took place later?

Your OAR Story Answer

_____

_____

_____

Evaluation

Does the candidate understand the seriousness, based on the scenario? Is the reasoning for the "why" logical?

Possible Questions

Does your current span of authority require that you make decisions that have an element of risk for your employer? How?

Your OAR Story Answer

_____

_____

_____

Evaluation

Does the candidate grasp the far-reaching consequences of bad decisions? Does (s)he understand the level of responsibility? Accept consequences?

Possible Questions

Have you ever had to make a "call" on a delicate political issue for which no prior policy existed? How did you reach your decision?

Your OAR Story Answer

_____

_____

_____

Evaluation

Did the candidate understand the risk? What factors were considered? Was the decision rational or emotional?

ATTENTIVENESS

Possible Questions

How do you monitor things that require your day-to day attention? Does your system work?

Evaluation

Does the candidate show awareness that details need to be taught? Is the system logical? Does it work?

OAR Story Answer

I've typed all of my yearly goals and objectives on a single sheet of paper and taped it to the side of my monitor. That helps me with the big picture. Tactically, before I go home each evening, I create a to-do list for the next day, making sure that the most important items are in some way goal related. I can also see how much I accomplished during the day and what needs to be carried over. (Sometimes I asterisk with my Palm, as well.) This check-with-goal system seems to work. I have a reputation of never missing a meeting or conference call, and most of my friends are always using me as their reminder of what needs to happen.

Figure 2.2: **Attentiveness Worksheet**

Possible Questions	**Evaluation**
People who work with you (and for you) sometimes bury information. How do you handle that?	Is the candidate aware that some people gunnysack bad news? How does (s)he deal with it?

Your OAR Story Answer

_____

_____

_____

Figure 2.2: **Attentiveness Worksheet,** continued

Possible Questions	Evaluation
Milestones can fall through the cracks, even when you're on top of things. Tell me about one thing that cost you something in terms of money last year? Lost time?	Does the candidate understand downside risks? Is there awareness of potential dollar/time costs?

Your OAR Story Answer

_____

_____

_____

Possible Questions	Evaluation
Describe a time when you tuned out in a meeting or conversation? Why?	Evaluate listening habits. If a problem, does the candidate have an action plan? Is (s)he aware of a problem?

Your OAR Story Answer

_____

_____

_____

COMPLIANCE

Possible Questions	Evaluation
Have you ever felt that a company policy was unfair? To you? To other employees? How did you handle it?	Check for resentment, bitterness, and/or "malicious obedience." Can the candidate comply even when in disagreement?

OAR Story Answer

Unfair may be a bit harsh, but when I was a new manager of inhouse sales, our comp people changed the commission structure, without any grandfather consideration. My people stood to lose quite a bit of change. Nobody else spoke up because it was announced as a done deal. I pushed—it really was an error. After costing out what was involved and building my case, I went to our Senior VP and got him to re-issue the plan and apologize for the oversight. Morale soared, so it ended up a wise, though at the time unpopular, move.

Figure 2.3: **Compliance Worksheet**

Possible Questions	**Evaluation**
What do you do when you have to work with management directives with which you disagree? Describe a recent example.	What comes first, the company or the individual? Which side does the candidate choose when there is a conflict?

Your OAR Story Answer

_____

_____

_____

Possible Questions	**Evaluation**
Have you worked in a company/department where policies and procedures were being changed constantly? What was the effect? How did you react?	Can the candidate conform, or is there a frustration? Does the candidate roll with the punches? Does (s)he understand that change is inevitable?

Your OAR Story Answer

_____

Figure 2.3: **Compliance Worksheet,** continued

_____

_____

Possible Questions	**Evaluation**
What are the company terms for promotion in your most recent position? Does the policy work? Why? Why not?	Does the policy work toward career management? Is the company passing problem employees from one group to another? Perception?

Your OAR Story Answer

_____

_____

_____

CUSTOMER FOCUS

Possible Questions	**Evaluation**
Tell me about the toughest customer you ever had and how you dealt with him/her?	Does the candidate practice a working philosophy? Is (s)he committed to excellence?

OAR Story Answer

I was put in charge of the Bratt account right after we shipped $200,000 of unusable product. The client was already demanding and demeaning before this, and he went ballistic—yelling, swearing, threatening to take his business elsewhere, etc. I dropped everything, flew to Delaware, and just _listened_. We set an action plan that included my periodic check with him and a hover tactic with our production group. I basically overwhelmed him with contact and information. I was able to build his confidence in our team and boost his self esteem, especially when I visited again just weeks later as well. He stuck with us and booked an order 15 percent higher than our sales rep forecasted.

Figure 2.4: **Customer Focus Worksheet**

Possible Questions	**Evaluation**
What distinction do you make, if any, between your external and internal customer? Where is your allegiance? Why?	How sensitive is the candidate to this push and pull? What is the financial issue? What is the political concern?

Your OAR Story Answer

_____

_____

_____

Possible Questions	**Evaluation**
What is your experience with customer surveys? What do you like? Dislike? How did you use the data?	Is the candidate skilled enough to execute a plan? Were the outcomes implemented and impactful?

Your OAR Story Answer

_____

_____

_____

Figure 2.4: **Customer Focus Worksheet,** continued

Possible Questions	**Evaluation**
Are there any negative consequences to the philosophy "the customer is always right"? Explain.	Is the candidate overly responsive to customer demands and too willing to change processes and timetables? How well does (s)he articulate a stand?

Your OAR Story Answer

_____

_____

_____

HITS (Hints, Insights, and Thoughts)

Once more, be mindful that every strength in excess becomes a liability. People who are genuinely customer-oriented want to help. They are dedicated to meeting the expectations and requirements of both their internal and external customers and use data to make product and service improvements. They build solid relationships. These same people, however, when overly zealous in their close support and eagerness to deliver, can be oblivious to important procedures and key manufacturing standards and may miss improvement breakthroughs. They can, in an effort to be "liked," also be supersensitive to criticism and defensive in their responses.

DEALING WITH CONFLICT

Possible Questions	**Evaluation**
What kinds of things upset you on the job? How do you react?	Does the candidate have a short fuse? Can (s)he bury anger?

OAR Story Answer

It's interesting this is coming up, especially since I just spoke to my buddy about that same topic. I'm not sure you can tell from what little time we've spent together, but I'm pretty easy going. I learned years ago not to get angry or too emotional on the job. I typically count to ten, maybe take a walk to change the settings, and stay calm. (It's also best that if I write my frustration in an e-mail or sticky note, I don't mail it right away. I save it for a reading later on.) The things that bother me the most are when people I depend on do not meet their commitments and miss a time line or don't follow up. I may be an accountability freak, but I do not enjoy it when I am late or not complete with something assigned.

Figure 2.5: **Dealing with Conflict Worksheet**

Possible Questions	**Evaluation**
Tell me about an interpersonal conflict you had with someone on the job. How did you handle it? What is the relationship like today?	Did the candidate deal directly? Was there an honest, problem-focussed approach or involvement with the boss? What is the concern for long-term alliances?

Your OAR Story Answer

_____

_____

_____

Figure 2.5: **Dealing with Conflict Worksheet,** continued

Possible Questions

What is the most recent "pressure cooker" situation you have faced? How did you react?

Evaluation

Does the candidate explode? Walk away? Give up? React maturely?

Your OAR Story Answer

_____

_____

_____

Possible Questions

There are always situations in the work environment that cause stress and problems. Describe one or two for me.

Evaluation

Can the candidate cope with pressure? How do the examples relate to the company culture? Is there a pattern?

Your OAR Story Answer

_____

_____

_____

DECISION MAKING

Possible Questions

What is the basis you use for making decisions? Logic? Intuition? Why? Give an example of your technique.

Evaluation

Are decisions hard or soft? Is there real decisiveness of action? How does that relate to the job in question?

OAR Story Answer

I'm probably in the middle of a 1 to 10 scale that goes from data to gut—say a 5 out of 10. I like to collect the information necessary, hear all the pros and cons, and come up with a numerically logical choice. Then, I mull it over, maybe sleep on it, and use my instinct to move forward. I used this approach when selecting a new software program for our database and ended selecting the mid-priced offering that eventually did the trick and saved us more money in the long run.

Figure 2.6: **Decision Making Worksheet**

Possible Questions	**Evaluation**
What is the hardest decision you have had to make? How did you make it? How did it turn out?	Can the candidate make tough decisions? Are the hard decisions postponed? What values are applied?

Your OAR Story Answer

_____

_____

_____

Possible Questions	**Evaluation**
What is the biggest career mistake you have made to date? What was the reason? How did you recover?	Look for evidence of logic and reason, or of impulsiveness. Are all the facts considered?

Your OAR Story Answer

_____

_____

_____

Figure 2.6: **Decision Making Worksheet,** continued

Possible Questions	**Evaluation**
All of us are at times part of the problem rather than the solution. Describe a time when this happened to you.	Did the candidate recognize the situation? What steps were taken to solve the problem? Is there evidence of defensiveness?

Your OAR Story Answer

_____

_____

_____

DETERMINATION

Possible Questions	**Evaluation**
Have you ever had to stand up and be counted on an unpopular stand? Describe it for me.	Is the candidate committed or just hardheaded? Is there enough "bend" to be a team player?

OAR Story Answer

That's a fresh one. Just before I left Dangle, we were forced to cut back on our benefit package as a cost-saving measure. It was my job to create the rationale for the shift and to explain it to our group at the next all-hands meeting—right around the holidays. It was clear when I started to generate the Q/A sheet that many of our employees would take a bigger hit than calculated. I went back to our CFO and convinced him that by postponing the change for just a month, we might get some "sensitivity" mileage and still make the numbers. No one was really very pleased with this recommendation, but it worked, and we got the savings we needed without too much hassle or mass grumbling.

Figure 2.7: **Determination Worksheet**

Possible Questions

Have you recently changed your mind on an issue after having taken a stand? What happened?

Evaluation

What factors changed the decision? New data? Adverse reaction? Internal politics?

Your OAR Story Answer

_____

_____

_____

Possible Questions

Have you ever had to do something that you know was right, but that would hurt you? Can you describe it for me?

Evaluation

Can the candidate assume responsibility for something unpopular? Is there strength of conviction? Responsibility?

Your OAR Story Answer

_____

_____

_____

Possible Questions

All of us face pressure to take action. How is this a factor in your present job? Describe how you react to this situation.

Evaluation

How comfortable is the candidate when faced with forced choices? How analytical? Does (s)he have the strength of conviction?

Your OAR Story Answer

_____

_____

_____

ETHICS AND VALUES

Possible Questions

What does balance of life mean to you?

Evaluation

Is the candidate able to carve out time for nonwork activities? What's important to him/her?

OAR Story Answer

At the pace we live in out here, that's an especially challenging question. I see myself as both working hard and playing hard. I try to spend important time with my family and friends—mostly on weekends—and define balance of life as working two jobs. There's one related to my professional life—where I am committed to getting things done—and there's another related to helping those I care about at home and in my community—where I am also committed to making a difference. I'm a busy but energy-rich guy, I guess.

Figure 2.8: **Ethics and Values Worksheet**

Possible Questions	**Evaluation**
What qualities have you liked/disliked about your bosses? Why?	Where does the candidate place honesty? Integrity? Trust?

Your OAR Story Answer

_____

_____

_____

Possible Questions	**Evaluation**
What would you do if you were asked to do something that you felt was unethical?	How much is the candidate willing to do to take a stand? How much will (s)he push the envelope?

Figure 2.8: **Ethics and Values Worksheet,** continued

Your OAR Story Answer

_____

_____

_____

Possible Questions	**Evaluation**
What does success mean to you? How would you assess yourself?	What measures are being used? How balanced are they?

Your OAR Story Answer

_____

_____

_____

HITS (Hints, Insights, and Thoughts)

It is really difficult to assess anyone's values and ethical underpinnings in an interview. A common perception is that you look up to people who are most like you, so in testing to see if you admire a well-valued and morally upstanding boss, the interviewer is assessing if you, too, might exhibit the same behaviors. Through stories, however, something like trust—defined by some as behaviors exhibiting *competence*, caring, *congruency*, and *consistency*—might be more easily elicited.

FLEXIBILITY

Possible Questions

Some people have a knack for being flexible—of adapting. Tell me about a time when you made this approach work well.

Evaluation

Can the applicant adapt style to the requirements of a given situation? Is the example given *really* a meaningful situation?

OAR Story Answer

That may be easier to answer now than it was a few years ago. I was the first HR member to join the BILLFAST Senior Executive Committee—almost handpicked and brought in by the CEO. About six weeks later, she left and was replaced by an interim turn-around type selected by the board. He lasted about seven months and another CEO took over. I managed to survive three different bosses and three different approaches and styles, all while implementing what was needed to keep the top talent from bailing from all the change.

When the company eventually folded, it was one of the original board members who called and encouraged me to check out another Senior HR spot at SWINGSWAN.

Figure 2.9: **Flexibility Worksheet**

Possible Questions

When was the last time you changed your personal style to adapt to someone? Describe the situation for me.

Evaluation

Look for evidence of general or specific style changes—whether real or related to the role.

Your OAR Story Answer

_____

_____

_____

Figure 2.9: **Flexibility Worksheet,** continued

Possible Questions	Evaluation
In any job, have you tolerated someone you don't like? Give me an example. How did it work for you?	How much insight is evident? Can the candidate really deal with individual differences? Does behavior really adapt to requirements?

Your OAR Story Answer

_____

_____

_____

Possible Questions	Evaluation
Are there times when you _really_ should not negotiate? When you should stand fast? Describe such a case.	Look for signs of rigidity or indicators of unwillingness to compromise if required.

Your OAR Story Answer

_____

_____

_____

GOAL SETTING

Possible Questions	Evaluation
What do you do when you realize you are going to miss a goal? Describe such an occurrence in your present/past job.	Are realistic goals being set? What ongoing performance feedback system is there? Are goals data-based or intuitive?

OAR Story Answer

Believe it or not, I'm pleased this surfaced. When I was at GOGETTEM, my sales target was for three new customers each month. The economy was still in the pits and not recovering as fast as predicted, and it was clear I would only make two in February, if that. Fortunately, my sales manager and I spoke each week, so I alerted her to the problem when my BLIND-MAN contact reneged on me. (She was obviously under the gun to meet our projections!) It seemed I wasn't the only one on our sales team impacted.

We ended up adjusting the quarter targets, and even though we reset the year, I still ended up making "rookie of the year" to boot.

Figure 2.10: **Goal Setting Worksheet**

Possible Questions	**Evaluation**
Does your current company/department have an MBO program? Does it relate to your own objectives? How well is it working?	Can the candidate define managing by objectives? Can the candidate relate goals to budgets and company plans?

Your OAR Story Answer

_____

_____

_____

Possible Questions	**Evaluation**
How do you personally approach goal setting? What criteria do you use? Describe a typical goal and how you derived it.	Does the candidate use specific tools or aids, or just arrive at goals intuitively? Is goal setting periodic or continuous?

Figure 2.10: **Goal Setting Worksheet,** continued

Your OAR Story Answer

_____

_____

_____

Possible Questions	**Evaluation**
Have you ever stuck with a goal after it became evident that it was a mistake? Why?	Is the candidate flexible? Is performance recognized as being more than just "hitting the numbers" or achieving profitability?

Your OAR Story Answer

_____

_____

_____

HITS (Hints, Insights, and Thoughts)

The Management by Objectives approach to motivation has been around for years. Research says that effective goals need to be SMART:

Specific. Something that is clear.

Measurable. Something that can be easily seen.

Achievable. Something that is within reach. (There needs to be stretch, too—not that easy.)

Relevant. Something that is making a contribution or difference to the process/company.

Time-phased. Something that has a beginning and an end.

GROUP DYNAMICS

Possible Questions

What is the best staff meeting you have attended recently? The worst? Why?

Evaluation

Does the candidate view meetings as useless? What mention is there of group dynamics and active participation?

OAR Story Answer

My former boss was a master facilitator and ran our weekly staff meeting very professionally. He attended a local seminar on effective meetings and began applying what he learned there almost immediately. We got an agenda in advance (time for each topic, as well), plus a purpose and desired outcome. He was gifted at keeping us focused (ground rules helped) and knew how to prevent us from groupthink or ramrodding decisions without getting everyone's input or capturing the diversity that was needed. I was slated to attend the program before the headhunter called about this opportunity. So many things go on when you get a group of professionals meeting every week that it's a key skill to learn.

Figure 2.11: **Group Dynamics Worksheet**

Possible Questions

In your current job, describe a situation where you had problems getting people to work together in solving a problem or finishing a project. Be specific.

Your OAR Story Answer

Evaluation

Was a systematic teamwork strategy worked out or did the candidate just "wing it?" Was the candidate firmly in control, or were the employees?

_____

_____

_____

Figure 2.11: **Group Dynamics Worksheet,** continued

Possible Questions

Do you think that participation in team sports can be helpful in adapting to business? Why? Why not?

Your OAR Story Answer

_____

_____

_____

Evaluation

Does the candidate see a relationship between sports and business (life)? Can the relationship be described?

Possible Questions

Have you had to work with (or manage) employees who were resistant to management? How did you handle it?

Your OAR Story Answer

_____

_____

_____

Evaluation

Does the candidate recognize the reasons for resistance? Which side did the candidate take? What approach was used? Was it successful?

✳ *Summary* ✳

✳ Understanding what motivates the question and how you may possibly be eval-uated can potentially enrich the depth of your answer. This can be especially true, if the question seems unnecessary or silly to you. You may completely miss its intent.

✳ Preparing answers in advance will make your real-time responses more powerful. Writing them down, memorizing them, and then practicing them is the best of all possible worlds.

MORE COMPETENCIES

What Else Is Your Employer Looking For?

Ask someone to define the word competency. It's seen as something you do well—something you are good at. The dictionary defines competence as "quality of being competent; fitness; ability." In your world of work, this can translate to effectiveness. What do you need to do a great job? What needs to happen for you to be the best you can be and to fit positively into the environment? The competencies that follow here, like those in Chapter 2, are universal and can apply if you are either a manager or an individual contributor. Again, study each sample and then fill out the worksheet that follows each, preparing answers that suit you.

INNOVATION/CREATIVITY

Possible Questions

What is the biggest waste of time on your current job? How would you change it or avoid it if you could?

Evaluation

How creative is the answer? If the candidate mentions "meetings," how would (s)he streamline them?

OAR Story Answer

We have a matrix structure here at OUTABOX, and I'm required to attend a lot of meetings. They aren't so much a waste of time as a waste of talent. I think we could use meetings for solving problems or working on key issues to improve our processes or to help our group gain greater impact. Right now we are meeting mostly to exchange data or just to update each other. I would recommend we use e-mails or even a quick group voicemail to pass on data and to meet as a group to work on real things. There is so much talent here that is wasted listening to information we can get in a different format. We can be much more creative and useful if we meet to make use of diverse abilities rather than just to pass on statistics or how things are going. This is another opportunity for that meeting management program that includes content on whether a meeting is really necessary at all.

Figure 3.1: **Innovation/Creativity Worksheet**

Possible Questions	**Evaluation**
Do you prefer to work with set routines, or do you like to try new approaches? Why? How successful are you?	Does the candidate adapt to a system? Use tricks from a former job? Look for new techniques.

Figure 3.1: **Innovation/Creativity Worksheet,** continued

Your OAR Story Answer

_____

_____

_____

Possible Questions	**Evaluation**
What do you think is the best new idea you've seen in your experience in the past five years? What is different about it?	Can the candidate recognize and understand creative work approaches? Did (s)he learn from the experience? Adapt it for personal use?

Your OAR Story Answer

_____

_____

_____

Possible Questions	**Evaluation**
What is the most creative thing you have done in your current job? Why?	Can the candidate adequately explain creativity? Look at the nature of the activity and assess carefully.

Your OAR Story Answer

_____

_____

_____

LEADERSHIP

Possible Questions	Evaluation
How do you delegate responsibility on your current job?	Is there true delegation, or are strings attached? Does the candidate delegate or dump?

OAR Story Answer

I consider delegation one of the most difficult things to do as a leader, especially if you are used to moving quickly and taking charge. My experience, especially at GOFORIT, says that delegating effectively also takes a bit more time than doing it yourself. I like to be sure I match what needs to be done with the talent I have on my team and to choose the right person. It also helps if you know your people well enough to bring them assignments that are of special interest or of a personal development nature. I was called away on an emergency client call and was unable to deliver a key marketing speech to our visiting sales force. I gave the assignment to the woman on my team who was a good presenter and who expressed an interest in getting more exposure and experience in front of groups. I went over the specs of timing, group expectations (big picture value, too), and desired outcome. Then I handed over my files and a sample PowerPoint. She took it from there and was a real hit—so much so that she was asked to deliver the same presentation at our regional meeting. I was thrilled for her.

Figure 3.2: **Leadership Worksheet**

Possible Questions	Evaluation
Have you seen managers abuse their authority? How? How did you personally react?	Can the candidate use persuasion as well as force? Is there a "joy" in the exercise of power?

Figure 3.2: **Leadership Worksheet,** continued

Your OAR Story Answer

_____

_____

_____

Possible Questions	**Evaluation**
What have been your major successes and failures as a manager? Why do you rate them that way?	Evaluate for effectiveness; consider the stage of the candidate's career, especially in failure situations. Look for maturity factors.

Your OAR Story Answer

_____

_____

_____

Possible Questions	**Evaluation**
What was the style of the best manager you have had? What made that person so successful?	Look for evidence that the candidate recognizes leadership techniques. Has/can (s)he adapted these techniques?

Your OAR Story Answer

_____

_____

_____

MOTIVATION

Possible Questions

What motivates *you*? Do you use those techniques on others?

Evaluation

Check for self-awareness and projection to others.

OAR Story Answer

I'm energized by learning. I do my best when I learn something new or apply a new technique or instrument. Fortunately, I've worked with people who have bothered to get to know me and either by asking or by observing have picked this point up and tried to build on it. When I manage other professionals, my first step at motivation is knowing, trying to figure out what rings the bells, and working toward it. It's different things for different people, once the basics are met. (One boss knew I liked picking up new skills and selected me to be the first to attend the Sorcher Train-the-Trainer. I, in turn, got everyone else up to speed. It was a very happy and productive time for me.)

Figure 3.3: **Motivation Worksheet**

Possible Questions

Describe the most motivational person you have known. Are you like that person? In what ways are you the same? Different?

Your OAR Story Answer

_____

_____

_____

Evaluation

Examine the "projection" made in the comments. Is the candidate aware of motivational characteristics/techniques?

Figure 3.3: **Motivation Worksheet,** continued

Possible Questions	**Evaluation**
How was your morale on your last/ present job? Why?	Does the candidate understand the factors that influence individual and/or group morale?

Your OAR Story Answer

_____

_____

_____

Possible Questions	**Evaluation**
Have you seen supposedly high motivators fail? Why do you think it happens?	Can the candidate understand/evaluate motivational factors?

Your OAR Story Answer

_____

_____

_____

ORGANIZATIONAL SENSITIVITY

Possible Questions	**Evaluation**
Have you been able to find out what it really takes to sell your boss on a new program or technique?	How well does the candidate read people? Is (s)he really sensitive to other viewpoints?

OAR Story Answer

I've been fortunate during the last year or so. My boss has been very clear about her hot buttons. She's a numbers person, so each time I want to present *anything*, I need to do my financial homework. I was determined to buy new PDAs for our sales team and got all my ducks in a row—discounts, upgrades, etc. I even called in a chit or two with my cousin who is the northeast regional marketing guy. I presented the options and got the OK. We not only saved a bundle, but efficiency in communication improved, along with two quarters of bolder sales numbers!

HITS (Hints, Insights, and Thoughts)

Delegation is one of those skills that requires a special balance. Many are afraid to delegate, are more comfortable doing things by themselves, lack trust in the talent of others, or micromanage and hover, without passing on authority or valuing empowerment. Others overdelegate without providing enough direction or help and set unrealistic expectations (or overstructure and limit individual initiative) for work that they should be doing themselves. You must remember to:

- Present the framework of the project.
- Describe the end result.
- Present the boundaries of time, money, and resources.
- Check for assignment understanding and commitment to goals.
- Review and discuss option deliverables—yours and the person to whom you are delegating.
- Set up monitoring and feedback processes.

Figure 3.4: **Organizational Sensitivity Worksheet**

Possible Questions	**Evaluation**
Have you seen situations where new technology has threatened jobs in your company/department? What happened?	Does the candidate recognize that technical obsolescence is a threat? Does the candidate recommend involvement in suggested change as a tool?

Your OAR Story Answer

_____

_____

_____

Possible Questions	**Evaluation**
Many communications contain hidden messages, and nonverbal communication is often the loudest of them all. Have you been able to read such messages? Give me an example.	How well does the candidate read between the lines? Is there evidence of being fully tuned in to communications?

Your OAR Story Answer

_____

_____

_____

Possible Questions	**Evaluation**
Is there someone in your department who seems to be successful at getting things done under trying circumstances? What makes that person good at it?	Does the candidate accurately assess the successful strategy and tactics used? Or, is it chalked up to charisma?

Figure 3.4: **Organizational Sensitivity Worksheet,** continued

Your OAR Story Answer

_____

_____

_____

PLANNING SKILLS

Possible Questions

How do you schedule your time for the busiest day of the week?

Evaluation

Who controls the candidate's schedule? Is there evidence of planning or of reaction?

OAR Story Answer

Every day lately has been my busiest and a real bear, so I'm not quite sure if I tackle each day the same way. I still use a Palm and synch it often with my desktop to capture what my admin put in. I always like to have my folder materials ready for my standing meetings and conference calls and set them out the night before. I keep a to-do list and match it to what I have going each day. I am often interrupted with spontaneous emergencies and try to take a minute between activities to avoid major overlap. I'm pretty compulsive about being on time and prepared so I like to give at least 15 minutes before the next activity. It seems to work.

Figure 3.5: **Planning Skills Worksheet**

Possible Questions

On your last job, describe a time when your carefully laid plans got all fouled up by someone else. How? How did you regroup?

Evaluation

Is the person adaptable? Rigid? How was the mess cleared up? Is there evidence of flexibility and resourcefulness?

Your OAR Story Answer

_____

_____

_____

Possible Questions

How have you set your priorities in your current job?

Evaluation

Evaluate the candidate in terms of near term vs. long range. In what context are priorities established?

Your OAR Story Answer

_____

_____

_____

Possible Questions

"Plan ahead" is a general slogan in business. How far ahead do you have activities laid out? What major items are on your agenda next week?

Evaluation

Is there evidence that the candidate anticipates requirements? Can (s)he change as requirements change?

Figure 3.5: **Planning Skills Worksheet,** continued

Your OAR Story Answer

_____

_____

_____

PROBLEM SOLVING

Possible Questions

Explain a typical problem that you face all the time and how you would go about solving it. Is the timing appropriate?

Evaluation

Does the candidate use logic and consider impact?

OAR Story Answer

I'm out there on the firing line almost all the time now, but my most pressing problems are with people and the judgment of a decision made. I am typically called upon to help with sticky issues around extras and additional fees in our service plan. A call comes to me when a rep is unclear about what to do or how much to provide without a fee. I'm asked in when the lines are unclear. My rule is to try to support my team first but to weigh the consequences of the long-term financial and emotional impact. I listen to the pros and cons—sometimes a three-way conference call is a blessing—and then try not to postpone but move forward without a big time lag. My track record is not bad either. Our group has kept the overrides to a minimum, and our customer satisfaction stats are the highest in the country.

Figure 3.6: **Problem Solving Worksheet**

Possible Questions

How do you feel about using a formal problem-solving process? What works? What doesn't? Provide an example.

Evaluation

Does the candidate see the value of a structured model? Is the example appropriate?

Your OAR Story Answer

_____

_____

_____

Possible Questions

Tell me what you know about groupthink. Give me an example of what you tried to do to avoid it?

Evaluation

How familiar is the candidate with problem solving in groups? Are there skills in facilitation surfacing?

Your OAR Story Answer

_____

_____

_____

Possible Questions

The world of quality/continuous improvement (ISO, 6 sigma, etc.) has impacted the way people solve problems in business today. Tell me about your experience here and what you learned and applied to your problem-solving skills.

Evaluation

Does the candidate have real expertise and/or understanding of the field? How does (s)he articulate the problem-solving approach?

Figure 3.6: **Problem Solving Worksheet,** continued

Your OAR Story Answer

_____

_____

_____

HITS (Hints, Insights, and Thoughts)

You can get in trouble when you confuse the cause of the problem with the solution itself.

A typical problem-solving process works equally well alone or in a group, but is most effective when you consider the following steps:

1. Discover and describe the problem.

2. Figure out the cause or causes.

3. Pick a solution.

4. Prepare and implement action steps and follow-up measures.

SELF CONFIDENCE

Possible Questions

Tell me about a case in which your ideas were rejected by your boss. How did you work through the situation?

Evaluation

Does the candidate bow down to management? Does (s)he go back and do homework for another try? Is (s)he persistent when right?

OAR Story Answer

Wow—that's so close to home—maybe just a month or two away, actually. My boss has a *real* strong bias against employee surveys or corporate climate work. He was a former HALer, where the data was often used as a hammer or as a club to come down on a manager who had serious interpersonal or performance problems. He only saw the negatives. I really didn't cave, but periodically passed on recent articles with success stories and wove in the fact that our key competitors were using them. I let others on the Executive Committee bring up the topic again and tried to add numerics to the positive result scenarios. He agreed eventually and came back to thank me for the professional way we implemented the program and offered feedback on the data. Two years later we were voted one of the 100 best places to work in the greater Philadelphia area.

Figure 3.7: **Self Confidence Worksheet**

Possible Questions	**Evaluation**
Have you ever had to sell a program or an idea under bad circumstances? Describe the situation.	Can the candidate deal with difficult scenarios? Can (s)he convince others? Change opinions? Does the candidate give up?

Your OAR Story Answer

_____

_____

_____

Figure 3.7: **Self Confidence Worksheet,** continued

Possible Questions	**Evaluation**
We all have to make tough calls under pressure or do something that's out of favor at the moment. Describe one for me.	Is the candidate comfortable playing an aggressive role? Will such behavior depend on the environment?

Your OAR Story Answer

_____

_____

_____

Possible Questions	**Evaluation**
How do you react when asked to make a decision in a vacuum? Without all the data? Tell me about a recent example.	Does the candidate try to get the data needed or just wing a decision? Does (s)he merely work with what is available at the time?

Your OAR Story Answer

_____

_____

_____

SENSITIVITY

Possible Questions	Evaluation
What is/should be the development plan (career plan) for the people you work with now?	Does the candidate understand that people differ in terms of goals and career needs?

OAR Story Answer

I'm pleased you're concerned enough about career management to ask that question, especially in such a small organization. I believe each employee needs to take charge of his/her own career. That's key. Nevertheless, as the manager, it is my job to help—to listen, to discover, and to remove any barriers, if I can. I like to meet one-on-one with each person who works with me to get a handle on what (s)he likes and wants to do and where (s)he might want to go next. Each person is unique, naturally, and I want to match skills and interests where I can. I always hope there's someone who wants my job. Bench strength is important to recognize, and I want to make experiences available that will help. My promotion track record isn't too shabby, either.

Figure 3.8: **Sensitivity Worksheet**

Possible Questions	**Evaluation**
Is body language really that important in communicating with people? How have you learned to "read" it? How do you use it?	Does the candidate seem aware of the importance of body language (that nonverbal communication is often the way real messages are sent)?

Your OAR Story Answer

_____

_____

_____

Possible Questions	**Evaluation**
How do you evaluate the performance of a new member of your department? How do you develop trust (or lack of it) in them?	Is the candidate specific or vague in response? Are the evaluation criteria used real or superficial in nature?

Figure 3.8: **Sensitivity Worksheet,** continued

Your OAR Story Answer

_____

_____

_____

Possible Questions	**Evaluation**
Describe a time in your recent job(s)when internal company policies had an impact on your job. How did you deal with it?	Does the candidate ignore politics, or play the system? How aggressive or passive is the role normally played?

Your OAR Story Answer

_____

_____

_____

TASK ORIENTATION

Possible Questions	**Evaluation**
Work pressures and demands can often alter relationships at home. Has this been a factor in your career? How did you handle it?	Measure how work may have had an impact on the candidate's home life; how home life pressure may impact his/her performance.

OAR Story Answer

My philosophy is to work until the work gets done. I am fully committed to meeting the responsibilities of my professional assignment first and then can get to my second job as husband and father who participates at home. My travel has not been international as yet, and I try to be home at the end of even the longest day. I sing in a local choir and am a scout leader, as well. Even with a partner at home who is amazingly supportive, I often have to choose one event over another. I am constantly balancing my time but am blessed with an energy level that makes most things possible.

Figure 3.9: **Task Orientation Worksheet**

Possible Questions	**Evaluation**
Do you have to spend too much time doing things that are outside of your aptitude and interest spheres? Give me an example. Does it bother you?	Can the candidate put aside personal interests to get the job done? How well does the candidate perform? Is it done willingly?

Your OAR Story Answer

_____

_____

_____

Possible Questions	**Evaluation**
Have you ever had the chance to literally design your own job? How did you do it? What did you put in the job? Leave out?	Can the candidate realistically describe the real job specifications and tasks? Can the person accept the true responsibility for the function?

Your OAR Story Answer

_____

_____

_____

Figure 3.9: **Task Orientation Worksheet,** continued

Possible Questions	Evaluation
How do you deal with people who have different skills and attitudes? Does such a scenario bother you? Give me an example.	Does the person "take sides" when people differ? Can (s)he work well with people who have a different outlook?

Your OAR Story Answer

_____

_____

_____

TEAM SKILLS

Possible Questions	Evaluation
What does is mean to you to be an effective team member? Give me an example.	Does the candidate understand team dynamics? Does the example illustrate positive behaviors?

OAR Story Answer

I'm a people person and have always enjoyed being on a team, even as far back as when I played soccer in elementary school. Being a member of a team isn't always a piece of cake. It requires lots of communication and a real clarity on what the goal is and who needs to do what to get there. It often requires you to let go of your own ego for the good of the end result. I was on one of the first cross-functional quality teams at CHRONOFIX, trying to solve a thorny distribution problem. It meant lots of extra hours and a continuous dialogue with a group of people I did not know well or particularly respect beforehand. We came in with a solution that saved the firm about 15 percent right off, and I gained a new respect for some of my co-workers and learned how to share some of the glory.

Figure 3.10: **Team Skills Worksheet**

Possible Questions

Define the word "team" for you. What do you do to create effective ones?

Your OAR Story Answer

_____

_____

_____

Evaluation

How familiar is the candidate with team nomenclature? Are the recommendations realistic and well thought out?

Possible Questions

How important is feedback when you are on a team? What can you do to encourage it? As a team member? As a team leader? Examples?

Your OAR Story Answer

_____

_____

_____

Evaluation

Is the candidate familiar with what is required to participate in an open environment or to create one?

Possible Questions

Tell me about the most positive experience you had as a member of a team. Why? As a leader of a team? Why? Which did you enjoy the most?

Evaluation

Is the candidate able to see the similarities and differences between being a team member and a team leader? Try to assess where (s)he is more comfortable.

Figure 3.10: **Team Skills Worksheet,** continued

Your OAR Story Answer

_____

_____

_____

TIME MANAGEMENT

Possible Questions	Evaluation
What kind of personal organizer do you use? How successful are you in implementing it?	How does the candidate manage his/her time? Is there familiarity with the latest technology or a reliance on an antiquated system?

OAR Story Answer

I'm just entering the modern age, I guess. I still like the basic Palm. I find it gives me everything I need, and I'm religiously fanatical about remembering to synch it to my computer and look at it before I close down for the day or start the next morning. Lately, I've been writing down the cell phone or contact number for the person I'm meeting, just in case there's a last-minute issue or problem. I also put project deadline and key report due dates right on the appropriate day, as another check and balance with my written to-do list. I set my watch five minutes fast, too, so I'm comfortable I'll be on time. Calendar integrity is very important to me. Meeting deadlines telegraphs efficiency, and I want my constituents to know that my time is valuable and so is theirs.

Figure 3.11: **Time Management Worksheet**

Possible Questions	**Evaluation**
Describe a time-pressured day. How do you cope? What techniques work for you?	Is the candidate sensitive to time? How does (s)he take advantage of the situation?

Your OAR Story Answer

_____

_____

_____

Possible Questions	**Evaluation**
Tell me about a time when you thought you would miss a deadline. How did you handle it? What were the consequences?	Is the candidate sensitive to the impact of a missed commitment? What does the example tell you about his/her time management?

Your OAR Story Answer

_____

_____

_____

Possible Questions	**Evaluation**
Have you ever had to discipline or provide feedback to anyone about time-related issues? What did you learn from this?	How serious is the candidate about time-based performance? Too rigid? Too easy going and forgiving?

Figure 3.11: **Time Management Worksheet,** continued

Your OAR Story Answer

_____

_____

_____

TOLERANCE OF UNCERTAINTY/AMBIGUITY

Possible Questions

Are you more comfortable when your job is well-defined, or do you prefer frequent changes in priority? Why?

Evaluation

Assess the candidate's need for structure and guidelines, and the ability to roll with the punches.

OAR Story Answer

Maybe that's another way of your asking if I prefer more of a start-up environment vs. a larger, more stable one. I can go either way, really. If my position is not defined, I do my best to create my own description and measures. I will set my own priorities if there aren't any outlined for me, or I do my darndest to ask a lot of questions. I need a certain amount of structure to be motivated. I've also been successful in systems where there was very little shifting during the year. When I joined a three-person start-up, I thought I would miss all the back-up processes. I actually thrived setting things up myself, with tons of changes every few months. We grew 100 percent the first year. Maybe I'm one of those few that can manage in either environment.

Figure 3.12: **Tolerance of Uncertainty/Ambiguity Worksheet**

Possible Questions	**Evaluation**
Have you had to postpone a decision when you really felt the need to take action?	Check for the "frustration index." Examine whether the candidate needs to do something "no matter what."

Your OAR Story Answer

_____

_____

_____

Possible Questions	**Evaluation**
During your career, there must have been times when you had to function without direction or guidelines. How did you handle it?	Did the candidate develop an action plan? What was the frustration level? Can the candidate operate independently?

Your OAR Story Answer

_____

_____

_____

Possible Questions	**Evaluation**
What techniques have worked for you to help manage frequent changes in your organization?	How has the candidate learned to manage the changes that occur in his/her environment? How does (s)he seem to cope?

Figure 3.12: **Tolerance of Uncertainty/Ambiguity Worksheet,** continued

Your OAR Story Answer

_____

_____

_____

VERBAL SKILLS

Possible Questions

It is sometimes natural to feel uncomfortable in dealing with people. Has this been a factor in your career? How?

Evaluation

Can the candidate speak out when required? Are there any clear indicators of communications problems?

OAR Story Answer

Early on in my career, when I realized how much I enjoyed marketing, I pushed myself to be more forceful and to speak out more confidently. I was a shy kid with a lot of good ideas, but I usually stayed in the background. At college, it became even clearer that I needed to speak up if I wanted to progress. I majored in speech and was forced, then more than ever, to over- come a lot. I am now much more at ease in one-on-ones, meetings, and group presentations. I was asked to be an inhouse instructor for the pres- entation skills seminar we purchased for our department, so I must have come a long way. I always liked people—it's now just easier for me to con- nect and to persuade.

Figure 3.13: **Verbal Skills Worksheet**

Possible Questions	**Evaluation**
What kinds of problem people have you had to deal with? Bosses? Peers? Subordinates? How did you handle it?	Can the candidate see the other person's viewpoint? Can (s)he work through issues? What kind of approaches are used?

Your OAR Story Answer

_____

_____

_____

Possible Questions	**Evaluation**
It can be difficult to sell your ideas. Describe a recent situation where you have had to present an idea for acceptance and action.	What is the strategy/tactic used? How well is the candidate communicating ideas in the interim? Is (s)he selling _you_?

Your OAR Story Answer

_____

_____

_____

Possible Questions	**Evaluation**
Some people say "timing is everything." Tell me about a situation or experience where your timing was good—where you were at the right place at the right time and did the right thing.	How sensitive is the candidate to the timing of communications? To the "readiness" of a group to hear good/bad news? Is (s)he really aware of the audience?

Figure 3.13: **Verbal Skills Worksheet,** continued

Your OAR Story Answer

_____

_____

_____

WRITING SKILLS

Possible Questions	**Evaluation**
How often do you prepare reports? How detailed and lengthy are they? Do you enjoy this? Why?	What is the experience level? Does the candidate willingly attend to this aspect of the job? Does writing come naturally?

OAR Story Answer

I should mention right away that I was an English major as an undergraduate and really enjoy the written word. Writing has always been easy for me and is an area of positive recognition, so I'm in my comfort zone creating. Lately, the report writing has been minimal, but in the past I was always the person who generated the first-draft report or the summary of the off-site and even weekly staff meeting minutes. I once wrote a department newsletter, as well. My articles tend to be accepted for publication, and I have had three books published.

HITS (Hints, Insights, and Thoughts)

A study of C-level executives using information collected from the boss, employees, and peers (now commonly called 360° data), validates the fact that the _best leaders_ are those individuals most able to cope with change and uncertainty. They are flexible and loose in style and easily adjust and acclimate to business demands. They are comfortable with ambiguity and uncertainty and thrive on taking risks that promote new and exciting vs. staid, same-old, and rigid.

Figure 3.14: **Writing Skills Worksheet**

Possible Questions	**Evaluation**
How active is your e-mail? Do you rely on forms or standard formats when creating formal letters?	Does the candidate fancy him/herself as a creative writer? Does (s)he have short cuts to help with writing efficiency? See value there?

Your OAR Story Answer

_____

_____

_____

Possible Questions	**Evaluation**
Do you set down in writing the record of important meetings, or summaries of action or important issues? Why (or why not)?	Does the candidate recognize the importance of documentation? Is there an awareness of "coverage"? Of future reference?

Your OAR Story Answer

_____

_____

_____

Possible Questions	**Evaluation**
How do you manage the processing of incoming documents? What is your system?	Does the candidate understand the value in retaining information? Can important data be sifted out and retained? Is there a coherent retrieval system?

PTOS (Practical Tips and Opinions)

- Underpinning any personal competency or ability is the *way* you execute. There are certain basic principles that apply to almost every situation that can help ensure your success on the job. In using them to craft your interview answers, you can also reinforce your ability to work well with others. Remember to:

    - Focus on the problem, issue, or situation, not the person. Be sure you do not accuse or blame. It only creates defensiveness.

    - Maintain positive self-esteem and confidence of others. Be sure you treat people with respect and assume they are capable and willing to do the right thing and a great job.

    - Build constructive relationships. Be sure you acknowledge that each person you work with has a connection worth establishing and maintaining (the power of positive politics).

    - Take initiative to make things better. Be sure you go the extra mile and don't wait for someone to fix something you can fix yourself. Speak up and pitch in.

    - Lead by example. Be sure you walk the talk and never ask anyone to do anything you wouldn't do yourself. Everyone is a leader and model for someone. Be a positive one. (*Five Basic Principles* used by permission from AchieveGlobal International, formerly Zenger-Miller.)

- Everyone learns differently. Some retain by writing and watching (are visual learners), some retain by hearing and listening (are auditory learners), and some retain by doing (are kinesthetic learners). Most use a combination of all three. Write your OAR answers first and as a minimum of mastery, memorize them or at least some key trigger words next, and then practice them with a colleague to hear how your answers sound and to be sure they aren't over-rehearsed and canned.

- Active Listening and really hearing what the company needs are key elements for success. (See Chapter 5 for more on Active Listening and non verbals.)

Figure 3.14: **Writing Skills Worksheet,** continued

Your OAR Story Answer

_____

_____

_____

✳ *Summary* ✳

✳ Remembering to include the results of what you did reinforces your ability to master the competency and could help distinguish you from your competition.

✳ Chapter 5 will deal in depth with the case method and "brain teasers"—two methods being used to test for both creativity and problem solving skills.

CHAPTER 4

TECHNICAL AND BEHAVIORAL OPTIONS

Certain professions and specialized industries see their needs as unique. Some financial accounting, banking, security trading, and professional service/consulting firms (McKinsey, Bain, Boston Consulting Group, etc.), as well as selective high technology software development companies (Microsoft, Yahoo!, Google, etc.) are wedded to hiring only those individuals with exceptional problem-solving abilities and heightened creativity. Part of each interview is usually a case study to solve and analyze or a brainteaser/problem stumper/logic puzzle to figure out. Interviewers use your answers and approaches as key evaluators for hiring.

Bench scientists, management and technical trainers, librarians, and often product marketing managers are required to do a formal presentation or a stand-up delivery. Some organizations encourage you to present your own research or to deliver on any topic with which you are comfortable and familiar. Others choose for you.

If these parts of the interview go poorly—no matter how well you do on the other questions—you are not likely to make the cut. Make sure you have all the information necessary to make your presentation and be sure you have an understanding of what your audience is expecting. Try to get as much information as you can about who will be present, how the room will be set up, and the equipment you might need.

CASE STUDIES

Case problems, puzzles, and presentations are harder to prepare for and might require special time, study, and practice. The hypothetical case problem might also come as a casual behavioral query—"What would you do with a client who . . .?" or "What would your response be to a complaining customer who . . .?" More likely it is a preprinted scenario that you are asked to comment upon and answer some questions. A good place to begin your preparation is to discover what the interviewer is really looking for.

Most likely, (s)he wants a candidate who:

- Can structure his/her thoughts in a logical manner (there are three things that can have impact here) vs. a shotgun approach. (One thing that's important is X and another thing is Y. Oh, I forgot to mention when I was discussing X that this is important, too . . . !)
- Can be put in front of a client without embarrassing anyone (i.e., a confident and eloquent speaker who makes appropriate eye contact, and appears both mature and professional).
- Can handle the quantitative skills necessary for the assignments (i.e., good/fast with figures and sensitive to the bottom line).

- Can prioritize actions and activities (i.e., identifies most important concepts and actions—the time constraints of only 30 to 45 minutes does not allow you the luxury of dwelling on unimportant items).

- Can use solid business judgment (there may not be a "right" answer, the issue is does the candidate make reasonable assumptions and reasonable business decisions).

Case Example 1

Set-Up

An old client of mine, one of the biggest department store chains in the United Kingdom, has historically done really well. Suddenly, over the last few years, its profitability has fallen off a cliff, declining 40 percent a year. It clearly can't continue much longer. You have a meeting tomorrow with the CEO. How would you structure your thinking on the problem? What questions would you have for him?

> **HITS** (Hints, Insights, and Thoughts)
>
> The complexity of the cases can vary and often depend on whether you are a recent college recruit or a new MBA with four to five years' working experience already. It's best, according to colleagues in the know, not to rely too much on business school theory, (that is, "Let's start by thinking about the 4C's: Competitors, Customers, Costs, and the Company." This just telegraphs too much use of jargon.) Also, avoid relying too heavily on frameworks. (A framework can provide some comfort in thinking through some options, but forcing a framework that might be inappropriate can do more harm than good.)

Explanation

Asked for an evaluation, the hiring management consultant said the following:

"What I'm really looking for is the ability to put some basic logic behind the declining profitability. Profits equals revenue minus costs. Either revenue is tanking or costs escalating. The really good candidate dismisses costs almost immediately—with a steady business like a department store, there's not much, practically speaking, that could cause such a precipitous profit drop. How suddenly and drastically could supplier prices or transportation or labor or real estate costs go up?

"The really savvy candidates quickly get to the revenue: Is it a price and discounting problem, or a volume decline, or both? They ask questions about where the stores are located, and quickly narrow the problem to the flagship store that's historically generated most of the profits, and about 50 percent of total revenue. Then, they start to work out what caused the revenue drop.

"Here's where the really good candidates open up another gap. The primary reason could be from the new competition opening locally. Some candidates will go down the path of consumer tastes changing, but how suddenly could this happen? So then we provide the interviewees with more information: There's been a massive mall improvement behind the flagship store, one attracting all sorts of new fashion stores, plus a new retail park including IKEA, has opened a couple of miles away. So the problem is widespread throughout the store. Then, we get into the practical solutions. Lastly, the candidates get a synopsis of what we really did and its impact, which was that revenues went up 60 percent after the store relaunched for the holidays.

"There are other ways to get through to a feasible solution. There's not one fixed approach or one right answer. For example, some people will start with asking how many stores are in the chain, what do the stores sell, what merchandise categories are causing the problems, etc. We're looking for logic and structure and a nose for value: Where are the opportunities for our clients? What practical things could our clients do?"

(Excerpted with permission from an interview with KBT, a hiring manager at Bain & Company, San Francisco, California, April 23, 2006.)

It *is* possible to prepare, to be ready for these case questions. Perhaps the best way is to study: Read texts that include practice case samples and reasonable answers, and then *drill yourself*. Drilling requires much more than just thinking about your answers or even writing them down. You need to find a buddy and rehearse. Hear how your answers sound and get some feedback on how you present and how you use your time.

Some of the consulting firm corporate web sites also include sample cases and answers, as do some graduate schools of business—Chicago's Kellogg School has its own Case Preparation PDF for example. Four books on the market also come to mind to aid in your prep.

1. *The Vault Guide to the Case Interview* by Mark Asher, Eric Chung and the staff at Vault, (Vault, 2005) is the best known and respected guide. It presents a practical approach to the case method interview and provides tips that have helped make a difference.

2. *The Fast Track: The Insider's Guide to Winning Jobs in Management Consulting, Banking, and Securities Trading* by Miriam Naficy, (Doubleday Broadway Books, 1997) presents samples that have been well received in the consulting arena.

3. *Crack the Case* by David Ohrvall, (Turtle Hare Media, 2005) provides solid advice from a former Bain manager on how to master this venue.

4. *Killer Consulting Resumes!* by WetFeet (WetFeet, Inc., 2005) also provides helpful case tips.

The Vault material expands on ten tips for answering business case questions successfully:

1. Write down important data. Take good notes.
2. Assume nothing. Take on the role of a consultant who needs information.
3. Craft meaningful questions.
4. Listen attentively. Take heed of the answers you receive.
5. Maintain eye contact.
6. Use your time wisely.
7. Prepare a structure for your discussion.
8. Think out loud.
9. Present logically and use a framework or business concept to help you organize.
10. Summarize your conclusions and recommendations crisply!

PUZZLES AND BRAINTEASERS

Sometimes high-tech companies hoping to cull for creative, innovative, and out-of-the-box thinkers make it a policy to ask short problem set questions to applicants. They pose puzzles or brainteaser queries that test your thinking and problem-solving abilities. Preparation for these questions can involve a study component. Reading and familiarizing yourself with the genre is a key way to improve, as is practice and rehearsal.

For example, in his article "Cognitive Reflection and Decision Making" (*Journal of Economic Perspectives*, Volume 19, Number 4, Fall 2005, 25–42), Shane Frederick creates three questions he calls a Cognitive Reflection Test (CRT). "The three items on this CRT are 'easy' in the sense that their solution is not hard to understand when explained, yet reaching the correct answer often requires the suppression of an erroneous answer that springs 'impulsively' to mind." The average correct score for members of the Harvard student choir group, which was primarily female, was only 1.43, significantly lower than the 2.18 average correct score for MIT but significantly higher than the 0.57 recorded at the University of Toledo.

The questions are:

1. A bat and a ball cost $1.10 in total. The bat costs $1 more than the ball. How much does the ball cost?
2. If it takes 5 machines 5 minutes to make 5 widgets, how long would it take 100 machines to make 100 widgets?
3. In a lake, there is a patch of lily pads. Every day, the patch doubles in size. If it takes 48 days for the patch to cover the entire lake, how long would it take for the patch to cover half the lake?

William Poundstone, in his book, *How Would You Move Mount Fuji* (Little Brown, 2004), provides tons of logic puzzles for testing and lots of practical counsel on how to ensure success. Some of his samples are:

- How many times a day does a clock's hand overlap?
- How would you weigh a jet plane without using scales?
- Why are beer cans tapered at the top and bottom?

Some of his recommendations on how to outsmart this puzzle interview are:

- Make the choice of whether a monologue or dialogue answer is expected.
- Discard whatever comes to your mind first. It's most likely wrong.
- Discount your knowledge of calculus. No more than a TV quiz level of math is usually required.
- Remember complex questions often have simple answers.
- Remember simple questions often have complex answers.
- Forget what you know about psychology. There is no perfectly logical person/being.

- List your assumptions to help when you're stuck, and then reject each in order.
- Lay out all the scenario options if key information is withheld. Missing information is not always needed to solve your puzzle.
- Try to generate an answer your interviewer has never heard before.

The Self-Improvement Newsletters provides subscribers with weekly brain-teasers—Brain Teaser of the Week—and solutions. Joining the group (e-mail: iqtest@selfimprovementnewsletters.com) and studying the examples presented are a positive way to prepare for these types of creative questions.

Some sample brain teasers are below:

- What is the only letter of the alphabet NOT in any of the 50 U.S. states? What is the only U.S. state with no letters in common with its capital city?

- Dr. Braintease wants to test your skills before he allows you into Math Club. Find the next two numbers in the series below , and you're in! 60 30 20 15 12 ___?__, __?___- Hint: The last number is not a whole number.

- Dr. Braintease came up with an interesting rule to develop the list of words below: Can you figure out the rule? If so, can you help him come up with choices for the next three words in the sequence? bash ring law ear go eel litter one rate owl ill ??? ??? ???

- Mrs. Astor's class had a birthday party for Patty the other day. Mrs. Astor brought chocolate cake and cut it into seven slices. Patty's mother brought a vanilla cake and cut into 12 slices. Patty is one of 12 students in the class. Half the students had only one slice. The other half of students had two slices each, and 60 percent of those slices were chocolate. Mrs. Astor and Patty's mother split one slice of the chocolate cake. Patty took home the leftover vanilla slices. How many vanilla slices did she take home?

TECHNICAL REQUESTS

Sometimes, in addition to case or brainteaser/logic questions, you are asked about a particular part of your technical specialty. The question might even require spontaneously diagramming a solution on an office whiteboard or fixing broken equipment on the spot. These are on-demand skills and are hard to prep for at any time. (If the test proves especially tricky, you may volunteer to perform the task as "homework" by offering to add more details to the solution.)

Read as much as you can about the company's plans or products and try to stay current in your skills.

PRESENTATIONS OR STAND-UP DELIVERIES

Whether your topic is presented to you or you are required to create your own, try to do as much preparation *in advance* as you can. Generate PowerPoint shells, hand outs that can be enhanced, and/or any other materials that can easily be adjusted or adapted. Your goal is to be on your mark, alert, and energetic, not exhausted from a last minute all nighter at your computer.

Be sure you know as much about your audience as possible: Who will be there, and

HITS (Hints, Insights, and Thoughts)

If you are unable to answer a technical question (even if it is a simple one) or cannot solve a case problem or logic puzzle at all, it is better to acknowledge the fact right up front, rather than attempt an off-the-wall reply, fumble and drop parts, or randomly guess on a diagram that makes no sense. A simple: "I'm stumped on that one, drawing a blank actually. Can we try another?" Or, "It's been an age since I've tackled that assembly work on my own—maybe I've been a delegating manager too long—so I'll pass on that, if it's OK for now." Honesty is still the best policy, and embarrassing moments can be a hard recover.

what their backgrounds are. Refer to your company research to discover any particular issues that might impact what you do or don't say. Stay in touch with your company contact to be sure you have some idea of what kind of space is available, what equipment it has (and you need to bring), and how much time you really have. Be sure you factor in enough time for questions and answers.

Assume what can go wrong will, so:

- Bring your own tent cards to help you with names.
- Bring your own masking tape—the 3M white brand is less visible—and markers (both whiteboard and water-based).
- Bring an extra laptop or computer link cord (and maybe even a spare overhead machine light bulb).
- Prepare all PowerPoints in handout format. (Color copies add a polished elegance if you choose to spend the money.) These are protection for equipment failure and should not replace the handout you leave for the group.

This kind of contingency planning may be a bit compulsive, but it is likely you *will be assessed* on how you handle problems that arise and how you work out the unpredictable.

Although these presentations represent a lot of preparation and work, it's significant to remember not to begrudge the interviewers this extended look-see. Try to view the experience as your first day on the job, knowing that if things don't go well, or even as planned, in the exercise, you've had a chance to see how your would-be peers respond and can gain confidence right away in the new position or bow out gracefully without breaking a commitment.

Again, practice and rehearsal add to your success factor, and your confidence is

> **HITS** (Hints, Insights, and Thoughts)
>
> Good facilitation techniques count and can make or break your presentation. If you can, set an agenda and some behavioral guidelines, and try to generate some participation with your audience by creating an activity that stimulates lots of discussion. Asking open-ended questions can help you here, too. For your Q/A, remember to respond and react as nondefensively as possible ("Yeah, I can see that . . ." or "That's one way to look at it, yet . . .") and to repeat the question posed so it doesn't get lost and everyone can hear it. "What questions do you have?" is also much more inviting than "Do you have any questions?" Also, as part of your summary, you can thank the group for inviting you and volunteer to get them whatever materials they might want from your delivery.

bound to increase if you have done the session before and have some idea what to say.

USING AN ANSWER MODEL

Some people respond well to using a format or a model to help craft answers. A format can give you a framework for a reply that is most likely to bring positive reactions or an answer that just works. Try the format below:

- *Take some time to reflect.* Ponder a moment before answering: Jumping right in and answering too quickly might seem slick and smooth, and a bit over rehearsed. Create a pensive expression, furrow a brow as you think for a moment. If possible, answer the question referring to the company's own situation. For example, if you have a success story about how you sold a slow-moving line of clothing, adapt your solution by substituting the car company's products and how you would market their overstock of parts.

- *Frame and/or position what you answer.* Frame or position your answer before you reply. You can do this by paraphrasing the question ("So you want to know my decision-making style—is that right?) *or* by making a comment on the question itself ("I was hoping you would ask about the way I manage my staff" or "That issue often surfaces when you look at my paperwork carefully.") The frame can give you a smooth transition to your reply and subtly connect you with the interviewer. It can also give you a bit more time to craft your reply.

- *Answer directly.* Provide a direct answer. ("Yes, I met my sales numbers three quarters in a row" or "I *am* fast on the keyboard—almost 90 words a minute now.") Give your answer honestly and as to-the-point as possible. If you can, try to use the exact phrase of the interviewer in your reply.

- *Reinforce with your knowledge or accomplishments.* Close with your metric result or accomplishment. ("The person I had to let go was so touched by my handling of the situation that she closed a big $200,000 deal before leaving. She did not have to do that. We then were able to make our budget number.") Let the interviewer know that you not only had a responsibility or performed a function, but also that you did it well, and in a way that could benefit him/her or the organization. It helps cement a positive view if the interviewer hears your measurable successes at the close of your answer.

Use your OAR stories here to sell. Certainly, humility and modesty are virtues, but not during the interview. This is your chance to shine and cite your strengths in ways others might not. If for whatever reason you think it is bad luck or too pushy or self-serving to talk about your talents, just realize that you have been specially invited to do so, and your competitors are also blowing their own horns.

- *Test reaction, if necessary.* Look for subtle cues and responses, if necessary, before you proceed very far with an answer (watch for facial expressions, such as raised eyebrows, open-mouth, or rolling eyes), ask, "How close are my answers to what you wanted or expected?" or "Are these questions giving you the answers you need?" This kind of "test" will help you shift your reply and provide something that will enrich or enhance what you have already said.

Sometimes, a quick summary at the end can help sell your point:

- "This example illustrates my ability to organize efficiently with outside vendors and to proactively look for ways to save money."
- "This story shows how I can create experiences that help change behavior and improve the bottom line at the same time."
- "Here my solid communication skills at all levels motivated the team to win the competition and bring in the new business."

Case Example 2

Question
Define empowerment. Tell me what it means to you and how you use it on the job.

Model Reply
Fortunately, I prepared for a question like that or at least something similar, since I've been living in the world of customer support for so long. *(Framing)*

I define empowerment as letting people make decisions, letting those who do the work decide what to do. It's a combination of delegating and giving your people the room to grow and learn from the decisions they make. My policy, when I'm asked to intervene or help with a thorny customer problem is to say: "It's your call. What would you do if I were on vacation? I'll support you as best I can." *(Answering directly)*

This approach must be working. My track record for staff promotions is pretty solid. Three of my six supervisors either were transferred to jobs with greater scope or were made managers while I was leading the group and the company was expanding. *(Reinforcing with accomplishment)*

Case Example 3

Question

What's been your experience with team-building sessions? What has worked and what has not?

Model Reply

I hope that's not a trick question, especially with all the publicity of the Pennsylvania courts awarding over a $1 million to the employee who sued her organization for inappropriate behavior at a team off-site. *(Framing)*

Actually, my experience is extensive. I've done a lot of team-building work. I've designed and facilitated at least one or two sessions each year for the past five. I refer to them now as team development sessions, however. It's a much more accurate reflection of what I'm trying to accomplish. *(Answering directly)*

My client groups are most satisfied, that's about 90 percent of the time, when there is a direct link between what the team is doing and the corporate goals or key initiatives. I make sure there is a direct correlation there and do lots of pre-work with both the manager and team participants on key problems/issues and the objective at hand. Setting ground rules, having a purpose and desired outcome, plus a participant-focused agenda with next steps and to-dos help bring results, and I don't just do them to do them. My evaluations are more than happy sheets and are consistently high, as I mentioned. Things don't work well and bring less-than-I'm-pleased-with results—that 10 percent—when I'm pushed to do work where the purpose is based on traditional, non-researched "we need a session on . . ." or when nearly all participants come with negative biases based on team activities in general. They hated previous experiences or attended sessions that just didn't bring value at other organizations. *(Reinforcing with accomplishment)*

That's a bit of a windy answer, I know, but I wanted to give you what you need. Am I on target here? I think team development is an important part of the job but does require more work than meets the eye. *(Testing reaction, if necessary)*

Like the other skills required for a successful interview, this model requires practice. Practice alone with a tape recorder both the questions and answers that you think will come up and those that do the best job of showcasing your skills and talents. Your comfort level at listening should increase with your confidence in answering.

Practice with a trusted colleague, spouse, partner, or coach. Videotape this rehearsal, if at all possible. Select those questions you might find sensitive or difficult. Once more, you will be able to test your listening skills and overall ability to answer effectively. Critique the video honestly, and resolve to improve both the content (what you say—the text of your answers) and the process (how you say them—tone, nonverbals, etc.).

PTOS (Practical Tips and Opinions)

Remember, your hire will most likely be based on:

- Your competence and skill in handling the job responsibilities. This accounts for 30 percent of the hiring decision.

- Your potential value and scope of your contribution to the organization.

- Your chemistry and your fit with the environment and culture, that is, your match in values, personality, work ethic, etc. This accounts for another 50 percent of the hiring decision.

- Your interest in taking the job, your enthusiasm about the assignment. This accounts for the final 20 percent of the hiring decision. Tell the interviewer you want the position. Never assume it's obvious.

- Remember also that there is a danger in *always* using the answer model for your replies. It can take away from the spontaneity of your interview and be a bit tiresome to hear consistently.

- Besides giving the correct answers to questions, there are many other elements to include. You and the interviewer should be working together to check the fit or future match. The content part of your exchange is the area you can prep for most.

- Be mindful not to bring Coke to a Pepsi presentation or Coach to a Prada interview. Those little things could do you in.

✳ *Summary* ✳

✳ Practicing cases and logic problem brainteasers is the best way to master them. Rehearsing with a friend is the most powerful.

✳ Staying current in your field and keeping technically on top of things will make the spontaneous "work this out for me" situation go smoother.

✷ Planning for stand-up presentation contingencies will make you "look" good. Practicing/rehearsing and preparing as much in advance as you can will make you "sound" good.

PACKAGE YOURSELF

Differentiators Equal Advantage

We live in a very visual world, and despite the efforts of the well-valued generation, a pretty superficial one. We put a lot of emphasis on appearances. Just check out the primping that goes on in many of today's popluar reality TV shows. How you look tells people a lot. Your package helps sell you.

YOUR LOOK

Your "look" during the job/career search experience, however, has much more impact than a superficial impression. It states your personal image. You want to be sure that your brand image, and the packaging to sell yourself, has a purpose and shares your primary message for your buyer. It is a significant part of the mix.

Today, consumers evaluate many aspects of the total product offering, and packaging is a key part of any assessment. Companies now use packaging to change and improve their product offerings. Consider, for example: a squeez-able ketchup bottle that sits upside down on its cap for easy pouring; a salt container that ensures a uniform flow in all weather conditions; a square paint can with screw top and built-in handle; a toothpaste tube that pumps; packaged popcorn and microwavable food products; plastic oil can bottles with tops that eliminate the funnel. In each of these examples, the product package told the consumer the product was new and improved, and this opened larger market segments for the items.

Packaging can also make the offering more attractive to retailers, especially the Universal Product Codes and accompanying bar codes that provide valuable information on price, color, size, and sales volume. With the new RFD chip, products can now be tracked at all times and provide even more key data on visibility, attractiveness, and usefulness.

Items that were once sold by a sales force are now available online or at self-serve outlets, so packaging has an even more compelling role. New laws make content and safety issues more important, too, and you now get more information than ever before.

Some companies even package their services: Consider the Enterprise car pick-up, Virgin Airline door-to-door limousine option, and the financial institution that includes counsel on insurance or mutual fund purchase. (Caution: Make sure the additional service doesn't inflate the price. In your job offer "service package," don't hide your real salary requirements from a prospective employer.)

What can you do to generate this kind of improved packaging and function in your product—yourself—if you cannot "leap tall buildings in a single bound"?

Today, a product package, including you yourself, must:

- attract positive attention.
- describe the contents and present information.
- explain the benefits.
- provide warranty and guarantee data.
- give some price, use, and value facts.
- protect the contents from damage, theft, etc.

Your job in this process, no matter your desired field or position, is to broadcast an image of confidence and competence—in both your personal look and your sales materials (resume, bio, brochure, business card, etc.). You want everyone you encounter to see that you can perform the work required and that you are the person you appear to be, both on paper and in person. If you don't believe this, just think of poor Mr. Brown, who misrepresented himself in accepting the head of FEMA role and was disgraced before the entire nation during the Katrina disaster.

As a consumer, you buy products that look attractive, such as the sleek sports car or the high-tech/digital watch. You also purchase products that look like they can do the job: Think of the heavy-duty vacuum cleaner or the easy-grip knife. Now put yourself in the position of your future employer, who on hiring you wants to show off the shiny new product to the staff and hopes it will work well right away. In many ways, the new employee is a reflection on the hiring manager. There's a lot to lose if your introduction and performance do not go well.

Your marketability always depends on good grooming and demeanor before your customers. As stand-up comedians say, know your audience. (If you've ever told an off-color joke to the wrong crowd, you know what that means!) So if doing your job well involves wearing loud, baggy clothes, body piercing, tattoos, and eccentric hair, make sure the job you just took is as a roadie for a rock group—not as an assistant for an investment firm.

The Right Clothes

Choose clothes that make you feel good, and that are both clean and well tailored for your body type. Much information has been offered in the media about determining the right color and style that looks good on you. Perhaps the most important tip is to choose a wardrobe that makes you feel at ease and good about yourself. You can meet a future co-worker or new manager at a number of places—on the soccer field, at a dinner party or at a business seminar.

Your goal is to look your best at all times. Mom set you on the right track years ago: Wear lipstick for a trip to the supermarket, clean underwear for the car accident that puts you in the hospital, or shined shoes when you rake the leaves. No matter what your size, all of your clothes should be stain- and wrinkle-free and fit appropriately. Avoid making any unintentional statement that flashes wild colors or exaggerated style—unless that look is your business!

Good Grooming

Stay well groomed, and accessorize without drawing undo attention. Be sure to take good care of yourself by maintaining your personal hygiene—shower and shave regularly, trim and clean your nails, and pick a hairstyle that flatters you and presents the image you want. Ponytails and scraggly beards, plus untrimmed and oddly shaped mustaches for men or long, unshaped hair for women may not work. Neither would four-inch nails manicured with happy-face images and/or rhinestones.

Make sure your eyeglasses fit your face properly. They should suit your image as well. The Elton John jeweled look or the huge, lens-take-over-the-face style might not work.

> **HITS** (Hints, Insights, and Thoughts)
>
> Any week could be your lucky week. Be prepared: your shoes shined, your hair cut; your interview outfit clean, pressed, and ready to roll. Have your day care lined up and your transportation secured, as well. You need to be available.

Fit the Company

As you learned in Chapter 1, Market Analysis, part of your preparation is thoroughly understanding the organization and your interviewer and effectively presenting yourself to fit in. Study as much about the company as you can. Use your network and make some calls for tips about the people you will meet. Check out business attire when you go to visit.

Your interview clothing should not only make you feel good but should also be comfortable—especially if you have a six- to eight-hour day of interviewing planned. While it is helpful to look and feel like you fit in, it's essential to present your true self for long-term success. You need to look current and at ease, not trendy or pushy.

Some seasoned professionals (over age 55) might consider toning up at a gym and/or coloring gray hair to look younger and more marketable. The color- or not-to color question is a debatable one. Indeed, there can be age discrimination. It is often very subtle, however, and is reflected more in behavior than in looks. Think carefully, then, about touching up your hair. It can backfire, if not done professionally, and should not be done just to get a new job or start a new career. Besides, a great energy level, fresh ideas, and enthusiasm for the job are the most powerful ways to present a vibrant and youthful work appearance.

Despite business-causal dress codes and even laid-back work environments that allow flip-flops, hip huggers, and T-shirts, it is best for men to wear a silk tie (color coded to an outfit) and jacket, and for women to wear a suit and dressy blouse for the first interview. (If the office attire is casual, men can always take off their ties. Be sure, though, to wear a button-down shirt so the collar and jacket ensemble will still be consistent. Angular, starched, and staid-collar shirts often stick out and rarely look very good without a tie.) Shoes should be polished and on the conservative side. Men's socks should match and cover the ankle skin, and women should wear stockings without runs. You want your commonsense professional personality to be noticed, not your latest fashion-sense creativity.

Remember to avoid:

- Loud colors and bold prints for scarves, handkerchiefs, and other accessories, even manicures, or inappropriate-for-your-age styles. Appearing vigorous for a job does not involve dressing "young" like someone half your age.

> **HITS** (Hints, Insights, and Thoughts)
>
> Test your interview outfit, accessories, and overall appearance with someone who cares about you. Be sure there is a high trust level and lots of opportunity for honest feedback and suggestions for improvement. Better yet, create two equally appropriate ensembles for OK/approval, just in case you are asked back the next day or even the same week.

- Statement jewelry—large-stoned bracelets or cufflinks, huge hoop earrings, dangling gold chains, four studs in one ear, and that 3½ carat diamond ring—is better for opera openings and glamorous occasions than jobs. This kind of jewelry acccessorizing can also mislead your customer and give the wrong impression, especially if you're a social worker with a caseload of less-privileged clients.
- Tattoos, body piercing, and earrings for men are still a VERY high-risk look in many work settings—and that includes an arm tattoo with your new would-be boss's name.
- Too much perfume or after-shave. If someone can smell it who isn't hugging you, it's too much. Remember, those with allergies will be negatively impacted.

NONVERBALS

It's important to be aware of your body language at all times. Sixty percent of what we say is communicated nonverbally, and you can telegraph negative messages unknowingly if you choose not to pay attention.

In general, you should always maintain an open posture and remember not to cross your arms over your chest. This can signal a closed approach or unwillingness to listen. You should try to give direct eye contact (shifty eyes can tell people you are hiding something) and avoid pointing fingers because that might mean an accusatory or blaming nature.

Your goal is to generate an equal mix of sociability and competence—right away as well as throughout the interview. If you are too nice, you will most likely appear insincere. If you are too task- and business-results focused, you will most likely seem arrogant and pushy and also overpower the interviewer.

Present yourself as a confident, self-assured professional—gracious yet capable. Appearance is your frame. What you say—verbally and nonverbally— and how you say it is your picture.

Active Listening

Hearing the company's wants and needs is the best nonverbal of all. You cannot sell yourself if you cannot hear what your customer wants and needs. Listening, in the context of a job interview, is often your key to success. Every job requires good listening skills, and even the most unsophisticated or untrained interviewer is testing for them. You need to answer the questions posed to you. You need to listen before you respond. You need to check, if you can, to hear what is behind the query to be sure your answer meets either the hidden or expressed need.

Look directly at the interviewer. Maintain positive eye contact. Looking away can suggest anything from shyness and dislike to dishonesty and lack of interest. If you need practice, try a staring contest with your dog. It will seem to go on forever!

Lean forward as a way to indicate your interest. Nod when the interviewer is talking to tell him/her you are engaged and connected.

Remember not to interrupt, rush to finish an inarticulate or incomplete question from the interviewer, or forget the question asked. These are the most obvious indicators that you are not listening. In our multitasking efforts these days, people have become ingrained selective listeners, so concentrate as you might to hear your baby's first words.

Use silence effectively. Wait until the interviewer has completed his/her thought and the complete question is presented. Typically, the voice goes down a bit when the thought is completed. Even though it might be very frustrating, let the interviewer finish those incomplete sentences and in-process queries. Some people may see you as quick and clever if you guess the right word correctly or complete the thought appropriately, but the risk in seeming pedantic is too great. A larger majority will view this behavior as anywhere from impatient and controlling to not listening and pushy. And never correct an interviewer unless it's to repeat a key fact. Any simple misunderstanding can be amended in your follow-up thank you letter.

Monitor your gesturing. As mentioned before, pointing and shaking a finger have judgmental connotations, but natural hand motions to pantomime an object or event can actually help the interviewer "see" what you're describing. Test to see if your movements are congruent with what you are saying, and remember not to fiddle with your pencil (much less chew it!), or scratch, rub, or shift your position unnecessarily. Your gestures need to reinforce your message and communicate both confidence and competence rather than distract, interrupt, or signal anxiety. The preparation mentioned above is the best way to refine your listening skill. You gather background information about the organization and the position so you can form hypotheses about needs. Typical organizational needs are skills for increased productivity, waste reduction, retaining reliable/loyal talent, generating creative ideas, solving problems, etc. You then match your skills, interests, special talents, and ideas to these hypotheses. Practice by describing your past successes and how you can add fresh value to meet present needs. If you are ready with your answers—both with your words and actions—you are most likely able to hear the questions and answer the needs in great focus. From *Understanding Body Language*, Geoff Ribbens and Richard Thompson (Barrons Business Success Series, 2003).

THE INTERVIEW PRESENTATION

When the interviewer arrives, introduce yourself and offer a firm, but not bone-crunching, handshake. A handshake tells something about you. It should be a confidence statement not an athletic contest or a "fish story." Practice with a friend—test it out. "Hello—I'm Shanda Lear," you might say, "I'm pleased to meet you." (Try to arrive five to ten minutes early, so you can acclimate to the surroundings and relax a bit. If the reception area has any company literature or framed awards, you might stand and "look interested" examining these at the time your interviewer arrives.)

Wait until you're offered a seat or the interviewer is seated before you sit down. Try to be seated at the same eye level or directly across from him/her.

Walk and position yourself confidently, with good posture and energy. That can illustrate both interest and enthusiasm. When sitting, you might lean slightly forward from time to time because this signals your particular interest. Leaning back a bit at times, especially after the halfway point of the interview, can show you are relaxed and comfortable with the interviewer. Shuffling, slouching, and stiffening up, on the other hand, can convey boredom, fatigue, or nervousness.

Open the dialogue by thanking the interviewer for calling you in. Choose from some of the topics listed below to break the ice and to make the transition to the more formal part of the interview easy for both of you.

- Convenient site location
- Contact/referral connection

- Ease of traffic or commute
- Office décor—art collection?
- Weekend recap (local sports team win?)
- Positive publicity reference

Note: This opening exercise has little or no bearing on the interview that follows, BUT it does give you a chance to relax and to connect positively with the interviewer in those important minutes of evaluation. It also gives you a chance to assess the type of person the interviewer is and what's important to him/her.

Speak clearly and succinctly. With moderate volume, use a tone that modulates both in pitch and inflection. You'll know this is working when your voice rises with passionate topics or lowers with more factual subjects. Remember not to speak too slowly or too fast. Slow speech hints at hesitation or lack of knowledge, whereas fast speech sometimes reflects the shallow salesman's style. Whispering or bellowing in either a monotone or "sing-song" style could bore the interviewer or present you as cold, with a flat affect. You want to generate warmth, often telegraphed by your smiling—and an upbeat manner. (Warmth is not easy to convey if it doesn't come naturally. Smiling does help, but not that constant, pasted-on, silly grin. Referencing the person by name occasionally also helps. Most people who appropriately reveal something about themselves through stories or anecdotes, that is, use positive self-disclosure, appear warmer than those who never share anything.)

Use language that is conversational and easy to understand. Occasionally, it's OK to use the buzz words or jargon of your profession, but don't talk down to an interviewer if you know they haven't heard the terms you use and avoid overly familiar lingo that might suggest an intimacy not yet earned. You do not want to seem stilted or arrogant in your delivery. And don't finish your interviewer's sentences! What you assume is about to be said may turn out to be something entirely different, so save yourself the embarrassment.

Show respect and courtesy and establish a rapport with the interviewer as you would a peer or close associate. Remember to be polite and not to patronize or become inappropriately familiar. Even if you think the conversation has gone very well, it's bad form to ask the interviewer out for a date.

Remember that this interview is not about you. They care about what you can do for them. Listening for needs means you reply in ways that show how you will generate revenues, increase market share, bring back a lost customer, or better yet, make your future boss look like a star.

PREPARING FOR QUESTIONS

A comprehensive interview can have from 40 to 50 questions, and there is no list that can include every possible query or reply, especially when it is such a personal experience. Check out the lineup of questions provided here and be sure you can answer them. They represent a cross section of information that will be of interest to the hiring organization and will provide additional insight to your "fit" into the group or overall organizational system. Remember, though, that the technical questions for your particular position must also be in place. (Chapter 6 includes an additional list of frequently asked and/or especially difficult ones.) In a well-planned discussion, the interviewer should talk about 35 percent, and you should talk 65 percent.

Your Professional Goals

What did you like about your last job?

Tip: List as many factors as you can that match the job you are seeking.

Sample OAR Story Answer
TOPSYTURVY was an especially fast-paced environment; at least it seemed that way when I was there. I really enjoyed the company dynamic and my co-workers. I also had a chance to experiment with some new technology and to work on the cutting edge of industry progress. I helped implement the paperless HR record system and saved us a bundle in the process. I guess, in summary, I'd say it was a fun place with smart people and challenging work.

Your OAR Story Answer

_____

_____

_____

_____

- What position are you seeking?
- What are your career plans or ultimate goals?
- What are your salary expectations?
- If you could have made improvements in your last job, what would they have been?
- What assistance would you need from us to help you achieve a good start?
- How do you show your anger and frustration?
- Have you made any mistakes during your career? If so, what were they? How did you fix them?
- Let's talk about "setbacks." How have they affected you and your family?
- Is there any pattern to critical feedback on you?
- What is the best career decision you have ever made? The worst?
- With the benefit of hindsight, what would you have done differently with your career?
- What three things could you do to improve your overall effectiveness?
- Where have you had the greatest impact? Describe your role in that achievement.
- What was the most important business lesson you learned in the last five years?
- If there were some responsibilities you could have skipped over the past few years, what would these have been?

Your Relationships

What do you want to be doing at work five years from now?

Tip: Try to present a flexible and open view of the future. The question comes up a lot for those either at the start or near end of their careers and is usually asked to test your commitment, work energy level, or goal-setting ability.

Sample OAR Story Answer
Wow, that question hasn't come up in a while. Five years seems like a long time away in my work world, but I hope to still be in marketing and to continue to

learn my craft. I wouldn't mind having a role with a bigger scope or more people to manage, either. The big progress in five years would be how much more I could know and how much greater impact I could have in my job contributions.

Your OAR Story Answer

_____

_____

_____

_____

- What kind of personalities annoy you the most?
- Cite a co-worker or boss you respect. Describe him or her.
- What has been your biggest regret in your relationships with other people?
- Who was the most interesting customer or client you dealt with in your last job?
- Describe the best person who ever worked for or with you.
- How do you stay current in your professional life?
- Why would you change jobs?
- If you were speaking tonight to the National Association of _____, which subject would reveal your specialty as a businessperson?
- What is the difference between a good position and an excellent one?
- If we hired you next week, what unfinished business would remain in your current work?
- After being with one organization for such a long time, won't it be difficult for you to adjust to another?
- Do you feel you have been successful in your current role? What accounts for your success?
- In your career, have you ever experienced a serious conflict of goals? How did you resolve the issue? How did you decide which goal was the more important one?
- What is your ideal job?

- Why do you want to work for our company?
- What direction do you see this industry headed in the next five years and where do you see (name of company) in this progress?

Your Management/Work Style

How do you handle difficult personalities?

Tip: Here is your chance to provide a general overview of your style and how you work with others, that is, "I try to be a good listener" or "I try to focus on issues rather than people."

Sample OAR Story Answer

In my world of customer service, I certainly have had my share of the "not-so-easies," I must admit. My experience says that people want to be valued and appreciated, so I usually do a lot of listening and try to figure out what's really behind the issue. I spend a good amount of time hearing people out and taking things in. I find if I'm nondefensive and adopt a problem-solving spin, it helps a lot. My old boss once said that if I couldn't work with Billy Badguy no one could. Patience and a bit of humor have also worked for me in the past.

Your OAR Story Answer

_____

_____

_____

_____

- If we could talk to your previous supervisor, what would he or she say about you?
- How did you prepare for this interview?
- Dealing skillfully with others on the job is important in being productive. Describe a time when you were successful in dealing with another because you built a trusting and harmonious relationship.

- Describe a high-pressure situation you have had to handle at work. Note what happened, who was involved, and what you did for problem solving.
- Give an example of having to devote extra hours to your job: when it was necessary to take work home, work on weekends, or work extended consecutive hours. Be specific.
- Many times it is important to be hardheaded about a decision you make, particularly when others don't like it. Give an example of a time when you stuck to a decision even though it was under attack by others.
- Describe emergencies or unexpected assignments that forced you to reschedule your work time.
- How are you best managed?
- How do you evaluate the performance of your subordinates?
- When and why have you fired people?
- What is the most adverse situation you have had to handle in your personal or professional life? How did you deal with it? What was the outcome?
- Relate the events surrounding firing someone or severely reprimanding someone. How did you feel about it?
- Note how your approach to managing an organization has changed in the last ten years.
- How do you stand on the issue of training people vs. getting the immediate job done?
- Compare and contrast the options for improving results through a salary reduction vs. reducing staff.
- What will you do the first month on the job?
- Have you ever had to implement a radical new idea? What was your success?
- Describe your experience in coaching others.
- Explain how you incorporate quality tools and best practices with your employees.
- What would you tell your boss is the most important thing he or she could say or do to support you?
- Give an example of a situation where a peer, boss, or subordinate stalled your progress and you felt ready to quit. What was the problem and how did you resolve it?

- Describe a situation that revealed you are a thorough analyzer and decision maker.
- Note a situation where you had to defend a position even though it reflected poorly on you.
- What would be the best way to motivate you for better performance?
- How do you turn around the bottom line of P&L?
- How do feel about downsizing staff? How would you implement this?
- How do you keep your boss informed?
- How much work structure do you need?
- What would you change about your boss? Your last company?

Your Insight

Explain a disagreement with a former boss. What was the outcome?

Tip: Present the focus as a technical matter or role clarification rather than a personal one. Explain, if you can, how you agreed to disagree and that your role was to implement the boss's decision. ("I gave input, but ultimately had to go with his/her decision.")

Sample OAR Story Answer

I like to keep the relationship with my boss as issue-free as possible, without being a yes guy and without caving into things that could cause long-range problems. As chief legal counsel, I typically report to the CEO. At one company, I debated long and hard about whether I should sit on the Executive Committee. My boss was more used to calling the legal group for help. I wanted a more proactive role, and did convince her that my contribution and value was key as a business person as well as an attorney.

Your OAR Story Answer

_____

_____

_____

_____

- How do you respond to criticism?
- What was the most valuable criticism you have received in your career?
- What have you learned from your job search?
- What is the greatest risk you've undertaken?
- What was your greatest failure?
- What has been your experience in working with conflicting, delayed, or ambiguous information?
- What did you do to make the most of the situation?
- What peer relationships do you prefer—those at a higher or lower rank?
- Describe a time when your understanding of the political dynamics at work was put to good use.

Your Values

What was the most difficult ethical decision you have had to make and what was the outcome?

Tip: Here is an opportunity to emphasize the positive and to give an example of your personal integrity.

Sample OAR Story Answer

That's a tough one, really, since I've been fortunate never to have had very many ethical issues to deal with directly. I guess I've always worked with especially honorable people who have set a clean tone. In the mid '80s, however, I was responsible for creating a process for a reduction in force—we had to let ten people go—and got a strong message from our leader to consider criteria outside the critical nature of the work in my decision/recommendation (who was primary family income earner, for example). In the abstract, this was a compassionate approach, but it was and still isn't really *fair*. I hung tough with job contribution, seniority, and work-related measures as benchmarks and eventually got lots of points for coordinating the most understanding and well-managed layoff. I bumped into the marketing manager we let go just last week at AMA, and he still mentioned how wonderfully he was treated and how fairly everything was done, and that was almost 20 years before rifting was a regular event.

Your OAR Story Answer

_____

_____

_____

_____

- What qualities have you liked/disliked in your bosses? Why?
- How do you balance your personal and business lives?
- According to your definition of success, how successful have you been?
- What was your most creative work situation? Did it provide financial reward, recognition, and personal satisfaction?

Your Leadership

How would a key subordinate describe your leadership style?

Tip: Remember to reinforce and build on what you may have answered in other questions (describe yourself in five adjectives, for example, or define a team) and establish a consistency in your replies.

Sample OAR Story Answer

It's probably pretty safe for me to give you this answer—I've thought about it a lot. Please, then, feel free to call on anyone on my reference list to validate what I tell you. Actions really speak louder than words in the leadership arena, but I bet you'd get an answer that would spell out caring and clarity as the hallmarks of my leadership style. I let people know where we are headed and what I see as the big-picture goal. I try to be clear about what success looks like and what I can do to help everyone achieve it. I spend time listening and letting people do their jobs and see my leadership role as making life easy and helping professionals do their best work.

Your OAR Story Answer

_____

_____

_____

_____

- How do you build a team?
- In your last job, what was your business strategy, your vision?
- What does "leadership" mean to you?
- Tell me what you see as the difference between team building and team development?
- What qualities make the best leaders? How do you measure up here?
- What two things do you do well as a leader, and what two things do you wish you were better at?

THE IMPROPER QUESTION

Many organizations spend time and money training managers on the legal implications of the job interview and tell them what questions should never come up—questions that are illegal, and if used, can cause both long- and short-term damage. The sample questions that follow deal with the seven classes protected by U.S. laws. This information is printed by permission from JHA Associates "Select the Best Training Program."

1. Age (people between 40 and 70)
   - _How old are you?_
   - _Can you keep up with the younger workers?_
   - _Do you think you can get along in our fast-paced environment?_
   - _You must have seen some action in Vietnam!_
   - _When were you born?_
   - _When did you graduate from high school?_
   - _When did you graduate from college?_

2. Marital status
   - _Are you married?_
   - _Do you intend to get married soon?_
   - _Are you a single parent?_

  – *Do you live by yourself?*
  – *Do you have someone who can take care of a sick child?*

3. Ethnic origin

  – *What's your nationality?*
  – *Where are your parents from?*
  – *What language does your family speak at home?*
  – *I detect an accent. Where is it from?*
  – *What other languages do you speak?*
  – *What's the origin of your name?*
  – *Sounds familiar . . . Isn't that from the eastern region of India?*

4. Religious preference

  – *What church are you a member of?*
  – *Is that a Jewish-sounding name?*
  – *Can you work on Friday evenings?*
  – *Are you a member of any religious group?*
  – *Haven't I seen you at the mosque before?*
  – *Is there any day of the week you cannot work?*

5. Females

  – *When are you thinking of starting a family? (Will you get pregnant?)*
  – *Are you pregnant?*
  – *Do you plan to have more children?*
  – *Can you lift 50 pounds?*
  – *Are you married?*
  – *Can you make plans for child care?*
  – *How old are your children?*

6. Sexual preference

  – *What is your sexual orientation?*
  – *Are you straight?*
  – *Do you have a wife?*
  – *What is your life partner's name?*

7. Disabilities

  – *What health problems do you have?*
  – *Are you always going to be like this?*

> – *Is your hearing good?*
> – *Do you have any disabilities?*
> – *Can you read the small print?*
> – *Are you physically fit and strong?*

Any one of these questions or others similar should not surface because they are suspect and subject to challenge.

Should you encounter these questions, you need to decide how to handle them. If you choose not to answer, let the person know in a nice, nontesty, not "gotcha" kind of way—i.e., "I'm surprised that came up. How relevant is this to the position?" Your goal is not to alienate the interviewer or to show him/her up, especially if you really want the job. Remember not to be lulled into a false sense of complacency either. You may be correct but can also be taken out of the running. If you have established some kind of positive rapport and are really OK with answering—not offended or wounded or see the question as just a way to get to know you or to connect—then do so.

This is, indeed, a signal or red flag but not necessarily an indicator that the person is a bigot, racist, or sexist. The interviewer could just be uninformed or not properly trained. Once you're on the job, you might meet with the person who posed the question and let him/her know the legal implications. This discussion will be invaluable but is not a first day (or before-hire) encounter.

FOLLOW-UP ACTIVITIES

No sales or marketing process is complete without "going for the close" or "asking for the order." Remember finding the "right moment" to ask for a big date? Or prompting your professor for your term paper grade? Closing a job interview involves just the same tact and timing. For you, it means ending the interview with information you need to move forward and following up in a way that ensures either an offer or a call back for more interview time will come soon.

Before you leave be sure to:

- Tell the interviewer you are still very much interested in the position and now that you've met and spoken, you are even more confident that the fit of your skill and their job is an ideal one.

- Resolve any objections that surfaced and end by emphasizing your strengths to perform the job successfully.
- Ask about the next steps if they are not clearly outlined, and be sure you have permission to call within the next week or so if you've had no contact from the interviewer.

After the interview, be sure to write a thank-you letter. E-mail seems to be the medium of choice nowadays—especially if the company is more high tech than high touch in the business—but consider that a typed or handwritten note might distinguish you (on classy stationery, of course, not cutesy notepaper from your kids' pad). If you live near the office, you might drop by and leave your letter with the receptionist the next day, adding another personal touch to your profile. (But be careful, as anytime you are in the office, you are subject to others' opinions. If you make a visit, wear business casual clothes—not your old sweatshirt—and be prepared to chat with potential co-workers.) Remember a thank-you note is a signal of graciousness—make your Mom proud that she brought you up "right."

Letter topics should include citing your appreciation for the interviewer's time, recounting key points of conversation, offering ideas still to be discussed, or clarifying any fuzzy facts. But keep the letter short and direct. This is a thank-you note, not a format to re-sell your abilities.

Try to send a similar note—personalized in any way you can—to every person you spoke with in your interview. If you only have the key person's e-mail address, you can encourage him/her to forward the thank-you note to the others. See Figure 5.1.

Follow up with a phone call to show you are taking initiative and interest and to further distinguish yourself among the applicants. Be sure to remind the interviewer with your name, ask for a search status report, and reiterate your intention in moving forward and staying in touch. There is a fine line between being an eager beaver and a pest. Keep your calls brief, and check if it's OK to call back again. Limit your calls to just one or two in a week; more than that will make you look desperate for feedback, ignorant, or insensitive to the interviewer's other work obligations or travel time. Think about how you feel when your mom calls more than three times a week to remind you about making a decision.

Figure 5.1: **Sample Thank-You Letter**

August 18, 200X

William Warrior
Senior Vice President, Human Resources
AZA
1300 Fraternity Row
High Desert, Utah 03476

Dear Mr. Warrior:

I trust yesterday's meeting was as good for you as it was for me. Thanks so much for your time and for the thorough explanation of your HR training position and life at AZA.

I was especially pleased that you appreciated the new benefits orientation I developed and delivered at BBG, and hope I can create something similar for your staff. AZA's mission and growth plans are exciting and motivating.

Thanks again, and please call with any questions or concerns. I look forward to hearing from you soon.

Regards,

John Youth

John Youth

Finally, review your interview and evaluate the results. Interviewing is like taking an exam: Sometimes you may have a gut feeling that you aced it or flunked it, but be objective. (Share the story with a trusted friend for another perspective.) Work on improvements for the next interview, if there are any. A note of caution: The interviewer's reaction might be hard to assess, unless you read minds or have lots of interviewing experience. Many are simply eager to please, fearful of legal retribution, or so reticent about discouragement that you may hold a false sense of success and never know what they truly thought of you. So it's extra important for you to compare various interviews and gauge your tactics and consistency.

How much did I learn about

- the job responsibilities?
- the reporting relationships/subordinate issues?
- the success factors for the first 30, 60, 90 days?
- the make-or-break skills that would ensure productivity?

How effective was I at

- expressing interest and enthusiasm about the work, the company, the team?
- providing specific examples?
- keeping my questions direct and clear?
- shaking hands warmly?
- speaking in a natural, upbeat, and well-modulated voice (articulating professionally)?
- appearing confident and decisive?
- emphasizing results that can contribute to the organization's needs?
- posing good questions?
- establishing a next-steps time frame or action items?

How do I really feel about the ...

- interviewer and future colleagues?
- the work environment and culture?
- the ethical stance and business values?

PRACTICE MAKES PERFECT OR PERFECT PRACTICE MAKES PERFECT

Vince Lombardi took practice to a new level. He is credited with the notion that practice is really not enough. You need to be good at practice to get the results you want, both in the world of professional sports/football or in the world of finding a profession or job you love.

Talk your responses over with a trusted second party and be sure the information is both honest and reflects who you are and how you want to be perceived. There are no right answers, yet you can provide all the right information and still not get what you want.

Listen to your responses on a tape recorder and test for tone and inflection and pacing. You might even practice in front of a mirror to get a look at yourself. Perhaps the best way to rehearse is on videotape. Work with a friend or a trained professional (independent career coach or outplacement counselor) and tape a job interview. This opportunity will be invaluable, especially if you have a real position in mind and can provide a job description to the colleague helping you.

HITS (Hints, Insights, and Thoughts)

Outplacement organizations often provide videotaping service as part of their offerings. If you have a choice in selecting options, try to include a mock video in your plan. If you are working with an independent career coach, try to select someone with video experience. Some firms re-use the tapes over and over again, so remember to bring your own blank tape for at-home review and refresh, one that is compatible with your home system and the equipment being used. Even if you dislike the process, push yourself. The learning is invaluable and especially powerful if you practice as close to the real experience as possible.

The video is rumored to add ten pounds to your figure, but the tape will also provide meaningful input on both the *content* (what you say—your answers) and the *process* of your interview (how you say it—your look, body language/gestures, pace, and tone of your voice). Your goal is to continue doing what is positive and shift what you see as needing work. One executive who experienced a mock interview as part of an in-company training realized he was unconsciously rocking back and forth. Another job applicant was able to see her never-wavering grin as insincere rather than the warmth she had been striving for.

You can never practice too much. If you can capture two or three key learnings that need improvement and re-do another tape interview with these as your goals, the chances of getting better improve significantly. Indeed, it is not the real thing. It is a setup; it is not spontaneous. Yet if a picture is worth a thousand words, a video is worth a manuscript.

Some additional tips might help make a difference in how your responses are received:

- *Use short, pithy sentences.* They focus on your results and accomplishments that can bring benefit to the organization. Remember not to talk excessively or explain too much. Make your setup crisp enough so the interviewer can ask follow-up questions for details.

- *Use language that connects you to your interviewer.* Listen to see if (s)he is using certain words (*think* vs. *feel* or *see* vs. *hear*) and then integrate these same words into your answers. Mirror also, if you can, the pace of delivery and energy level. Also, remember not to use "we" in referring to your former organization. It might obscure what you did to help your former employer succeed. Instead, use "we" when referring to what you plan to do on the new job. This is leverage designed to help the interviewer see you as already part of the team. It also strengthens your personal involvement and successes.

- *Use your time wisely.* Remember not to ramble, pontificate, or reminisce. Get to your point quickly. But there's no need to remind the interviewer of the time, especially in a serial interview session. The courtesy you extend may cut short a good interview or imply that you, not the interviewer, are controlling the clock.

- *Use discretion at all times.* Remember not to gossip or to speak negatively about your former boss or organization.

> ## HITS (Hints, Insights, and Thoughts)
>
> Assume there is a logical reason for every question asked. Knowing the motivation behind the query and how it relates to the specific position will help you craft the appropriate answer. For example, a salesperson needs to deal with rejection, so a question about handling disappointment might include something about your knowing when to move on from an unreasonable deal or your ability at rebounding once you have analyzed what might have gone wrong or what you can learn from the encounter.

PTOS (Practical Tips and Opinions)

- Come a few minutes early for your interview. Remember not to cut it too close or be a little late. (Even if you arrive at the building on time, if the receptionist is slow and it takes a while to locate your contact, you could be judged "late.") Give yourself enough time to dry off or freshen up if coming into the office from a downpour or snowstorm.

- At meeting and departure contact, be sure to shake hands with each person in your panel or group interview. Get a business card from each person, if you can.

- Bring along some energy bar snacks for boosts during an all-day interview when there might not be breaks to eat.

- Bring a PDA with you to the interview. It can suggest you're computer-savvy and comfortable with technology, and perhaps dispel an older image.

- Try to schedule your interviews in the morning, when most people are fresh and alert. Avoid Mondays and Fridays, if at all possible, and book your spot at the end of the candidate cue, last if you can. (Those interviewed last (56 percent) vs. first (14 percent) obtained the most job offers. It's perhaps an indication that busy interviewers tend to remember those most immediate in their thoughts.

- Soften negative or inflammatory words by re-crafting them in a positive tone. Remember not to repeat a negative term back to the interviewer—turn "weakness" into "area of improvement" or "something to master"; "failure" to "things could have turned out differently"; "regret" to "I wish it had turned out better"; or "conflict" to "issues" or "challenges."

- You can be safe if you dress most professionally (men in ties and jackets; women in business suits) the very *first* time you meet someone at the organization, even on casual Friday. You can always dress down at the moment or get more casual to fit in when you are asked to return. Dressing up is much harder. (In years past, the rule used to be to dress for two levels above the person interviewing you.)

✴ *Summary* ✴

✴ Creating a positive first impression is paramount, especially when some theorists think the like/dislike decision is made after just a few seconds. You can't tell a book by its cover, but you may be tempted to buy it if the cover looks attractive.

✴ Answering the questions appropriately requires the ability to understand, to listen, to look, and to balance what's going on at the moment. There is often no real right answer but the one that fits you and matches what the hiring manager and the organization is looking for. Practice, practice, practice.

✴ Being prepared for an improper or illegal question can help.

✴ Monitoring your nonverbals and those of your interviewer is important because it telegraphs a lot of important information.

✴ Following up appropriately is a key step no matter what the result.

THE RISKS OF
YOUR REPLIES

The answers you provide in an interview are especially personal and need to reveal who you are and how you can help the organization. A canned, memorized reply can only come back to haunt you. There is no list that can anticipate every possible reply, but check out the lineup in this chapter of questions and answers that reflect the more common and standard interrogations, as well as the sticklers and tough ones.

Remember the most positive (and skillful) interviewer is searching for red flags, any misstatements, contradictions, or extreme views, that would probably disqualify you right away. (S)he knows more about the position, the cast of characters, and the organization than you do, so the questions, if crafted properly, are used to see how you match the requirements and environment. You must be honest and forthcoming. You cannot lie or misrepresent yourself.

No, not even a white lie—the kind many use to rename position titles, dates of employment, salary, or grade point averages. Lies are false pretenses with troublesome consequences. The risks of dismissal are too great. You can trigger a negative reaction. You can inadvertently wreck your chances. You can lose the offer or fail miserably at the position if you are lucky enough to land it. High-profile sports coaches, banking executives, and well-backed politicians may be long into their careers when a lie on their resume is discovered and they are fired in a humiliating fashion (making it that much harder to gain the trust of another hiring manager).

DESCRIPTORS

Tell me about yourself. (Describe yourself for me.)

Tip: This lead question could be your biggest chance to win over your interviewer and often comes at the start of your time together. Here is an opportunity to illustrate both your sociability and competency components. Be careful not to fluster, filibuster, or familiarize. If you are not prepared, talk too long, or get too personal, you will lose the interviewer's interest early and the substance of your following replies—however purposeful—will be lost to deaf ears. You need to be seen as prepared and focused.

Some job seekers prepare a 60-second "elevator speech" or "infomercial" that explains what they do and the kind of skills they have to do it. You can use the ingredients of your infomercial here, as well, but start with a clarification:

"Let me begin by telling you about my professional self first."

You can steer the interviewer to your resume next.

"As you can see from my resume . . . ."

You can then explain your education and describe your best work from position to position:

"I got my B.S. in Accounting from Babson and then went directly to _____ (FACT) where I_____. One year after I was promoted, my former boss recruited me to _____ (INSIGHT)_, where I_____, etc." (Once again, use action words to describe what you did and strong descriptors to describe how you did it.)

You can finish by emphasizing a winning accomplishment from your last position:

"I'm most proud of the XY project I set up at SIGNAL. Here I_____"

You can summarize and close with your interest to continue the relationship:

"So that's me at work. Later, I'd enjoy telling you about how my job pursuits are also reflected in my personal interests."

Sample OAR Story Answer

I thought you'd want to know about this, so let me highlight my resume and tell you first about my key professional work experience after completing my formal education. I have___(7)_____years' professional experience as an ____(accountant)_____in the____(retail)_____industry, specializing in__(men's accessories)____ and _____(outdoor wear)_____.

One accomplishment that makes me proud was finalized just recently at_____(Banana Republic)_____. My___(work on an inventory management plan)_____ resulted in __(saving $10,000 in the first quarter alone. ___ %; # of hours, days, times, rank, products, accounts, items, customers, sales, reliability, durability, accuracy, repeat business, etc.)_____.

HITS (Hints, Insights, and Thoughts)

Remember, a job interview is not confession. You are not on a one-on-one with your religious leader. Reveal and report what puts you in a positive light—only appropriate information and data that is requested, not unsolicited or volunteered information that could ultimately lose you an offer. The interview is not a time for disclosing your dirty laundry.

In addition, I'm a New England native and have a (AA, BS, MA, Ph.D., certificate, license, degree) in_____(Accounting)_____ from the College of_____(the Pacific)_____in_____(Stockton)_____.

There's more of my work interest also expressed in my personal life; if you'd like, I can share more about this at a later time.

Your OAR Story Answer

_____

_____

_____

_____

AVAILABILITY

Why did you leave your last position?

Tip: Feel free to rely on your "reason for availability," a statement you crafted at the beginning of your search process (see *Hire Me, Inc.*, Entrepreneur Press, Chapter 1). Be positive. Be brief. Remember there's no need to provide too many details or to dwell on sensitive or emotional-baggage issues. The country music hit song lyric says it well, "That's my story and I'm stickin' to it!"

Sample OAR Story Answer

"Our entire group was eliminated when the organization restructured. It was purely a business decision where many of the company's top employees were impacted."

Your OAR Story Answer

_____

_____

_____

_____

RIGHT FOR THE POSITION?

Why should we hire you?

Tip: Be clear that not only can you do the job but you also want to do it. There's no need to be coy or humble. You should stress that you know how to do what is needed to get the job done and your qualifications meet the requirements.

Sample OAR Story Answer

"I'm pleased you included that question. I'm encouraged by the near-ideal fit for what you need to do and what I'm successful at doing. This match motivates me to apply my proven skills to achieving the tasks you have in mind for the role here. I'm interested in working at BOXES and striking this match to flame."

Your OAR Story Answer

_____

_____

_____

_____

STRENGTHS

What are your strengths?

Tip: In your self-assessment work from Chapter 1, you put some effort into preparing for this question. Try to select a work-related positive that is of particular value to the position, team, or organization. Provide one right away, but ask if the interviewer wants another and have it ready.

Sample OAR Story Answer

"I'm pretty lucky to have a few positive things I'm proud of. I'll pick one for right now, but let me know if you'd like more. My people skills are always singled out at review time. I try to treat people respectfully, no matter where they fit into the organization, and resolve issues directly before they fester. That style probably saves a lot of churning of decisions and downtime when problems come up. At HIGHTOP's sales convention a year ago, I even won the Most Cooperative Engineer award.

Your OAR Story Answer

_____

_____

_____

_____

DESCRIPTORS

Describe yourself in five adjectives.

Tip: Here, once more, is your chance to position yourself for what the job might require or for what you've learned the organization likes its employees to have. It also gives you a chance to present an honest view of who you really are. Be sure to provide a variety of descriptors that cover a range of skills, rather than selecting words that mean the same thing: "Dedicated" is almost the same as "committed" and "hard working," and "humorous" is almost the same as "fun-loving." Choose words that represent you accurately. If you are quiet and reserved, do not say "upbeat" and "perky." It won't fit, and it will be obvious you're giving an answer you think (s)he wants to hear or is required for the job. The astute interviewer is testing not only to see if you know what an adjective really is ("people-oriented" is an adjective, "people person" is a noun, "relates well to people" is an action) but also for congruency—how (s)he sees you vs. how you see yourself.

Sample OAR Story Answer
Let's see: "I'm positive, task-oriented, creative, collaborative, and committed . . . to bottom line results."

Your OAR Story Answer

_____

_____

_____

_____

WEAKNESSES

What are your weaknesses?

Tip: Try to admit to a weakness that's not directly related to a core competency. But be mindful that many interviewers are now tuned in to the weakness-that-some-consider-a-strength approach: "I work too hard" or "I'm too much of a perfectionist."

You're probably safe noting a weakness related to your work style, one not connected to the job role you're seeking, i.e., a software engineer or a bench chemist might disclose that (s)he is not a terrific public speaker and needs work there. A shortcoming you were told about early in your career and have now mastered, or a generic glitch that everyone can work harder to overcome (such as with more computer or technical training or enhanced presentation skills, etc.), are options to use.

Sample OAR Story Answer

"No one is perfect, of course. Everyone can get better at something—I certainly know that. Early in my career as a manager, I was told I needed improvement in delegating assignments. I kept on loading not-so-challenging work on only those who asked or volunteered for it. I took an inhouse training course called the "Art of Delegation" and focused on asking better questions and matching skills to interests more. It must have worked—now I usually get super ratings when employees are surveyed on how well their manager delegates.

Your OAR Story Answer

_____

_____

_____

_____

CRITIQUES BY BOSSES

What negatives would your last boss have to say about you?

Tip: This can be a tricky question (one with a trap for you to fall into), especially if you were asked for additional weaknesses or areas for improvement earlier in the interview (i.e., IN WHAT THREE AREAS COULD YOU BE MORE PRODUCTIVE AS AN EMPLOYEE? or WHAT ARE YOUR WEAKNESSES?). Again, use the same guidelines presented above, but remember that only two or three weaknesses should surface for the entire interview. An artful interviewer will ask for improvement areas in many different ways, hoping you will pile up a list.

Sample OAR Story Answer

"My boss would have mostly nice things to say about me; but if pressed, she might say I short-shrifted myself in professional development. I have applied for at least two seminars each year, but cancelled all of them at the last minute when my work got extra busy. She urges personal growth and wanted me to find a way to attend the seminars. I'm sure I disappointed her.

Your OAR Story Answer

_____

_____

_____

_____

SALARY REQUIREMENTS

What are your salary expectations?

Tip: Tossing out a salary number without knowing the industry wage range or what the organization pays for that role can put you in either the overqualified or bargain-basement candidate category. If you've ever purchased a new car, you know the salesperson often asks, "What do you want to pay?" which is like asking, "How much do you have in your bank account?" In short, if you know the fair market value for the role, you can negotiate prudently and in good faith. See if you can determine the compensation range of the position beforehand.

Many web sites in your industry such as www.sixfigurejobs.com, www.wageweb.com, wwwjobstar.org, www.salarysource.com, and www.salary.com, can give you this value range. Look them up, and then give your acceptable range, if pressed further for a reply. If you ask, some interviewers will tell you the range then, and you can verbalize if it's acceptable. Finally, you need to be honest and straight-talking if the interviewer asks you directly for an earnings history or for the exact dollar amount of your base pay, bonus, or total compensation where you worked most recently.

Remember also to avoid statements that can come back to haunt you when you start salary negotiations later on. "Money isn't important to me right now" or "I really don't need very much to live on." (You're independently wealthy and would perform this job for free as a public service?)

Sample OAR Story Answer

"My expectations right now are open, and I certainly take into consideration the entire compensation package, not

---

HITS (Hints, Insights, and Thoughts)

Listen carefully to the wording of the salary question. There is a difference between "What are your salary expectations?" and "What was your base pay at HOPSCOTCH?"

The first gives you a chance to position or to ferret out the existing range before providing an acceptable number. The second deserves a direct response. In each case, you do have the option, however, of citing any additional money made via an incentive bonus, sign-on fee, freelance pay or consulting compensation for your complete salary. (Note that most company HR reps now, if asked for your salary figure, are required to withhold the information, confirming only your dates of employment and job titles.)

just base pay. I did do some research on salary ranges and what Springfield companies are now paying for this work. You have a strong reputation, and I'm sure you, too, are paying fairly for the position. How have you set the range?"

Your OAR Story Answer

_____

_____

_____

_____

COMPANY KNOWLEDGE

What do you know about this company?

Tip: Now is your chance to draw on the research you did to prepare and wow the interviewer with the data you were able to uncover and inside information you learned. If this question does not come up, try to weave some of this knowledge into your other answers. Let the interviewer know you did your homework (and that the dog didn't eat it this time).

Sample OAR Story Answer
"Thanks for bringing this up now because it will remind me of some questions I have for you later. I did spend some time studying your web site and reading both your annual report and your NINEX product brochure. I also picked Brenda Zass' brain about what the environment was really like and how the organization really functioned. I learned a lot and validated what I thought when I singled you out as a target organization—you have a great reputation as a strong industry leader, a large and growing share of the market, a respected product, and a fun, if not pressured, and task-oriented working culture."

Your OAR Story Answer

_____

_____

_____

_____

QUALIFICATIONS

Why do you feel qualified for this position?

Tip: No need to be shy or hesitant with this question. You would never have gotten to the interview if you did not have the qualifications or skills to do the job. Look back to your achievements and OAR stories and try to position your answers to satisfy the organization's needs. Link what you know about the job with the facts you know about the company's problems.

Sample OAR Story Answer
"I've been fortunate enough in my last two positions to have created award-winning customer service groups. You were candid enough when we first spoke on the phone to acknowledge that WEEDERS needed to improve its product support and regain some of the customers lost. I'm confident I can apply the techniques that have worked before here and make a major contribution to getting you what you need. I've done it before and I can do it here."

Your OAR Story Answer

_____

_____

_____

_____

SIGNIFICANT BUSINESS ACHIEVEMENT

What's been your most significant business achievement to date and why are you telling me this one?

Tip: Remember to select an example that best relates to this organization and/or the particular job at hand and provide a brief executive summary, so the interviewer can ask for a longer version or more details if necessary. Your reason for this selection can certainly be your personal learning or satisfaction/reward, but it is better focused if the company will benefit: "I can do the same thing for you here."

Sample OAR Story Answer

"My career is filled with many wonderful successes, but if I'm asked for just one it would be the creation of a career management program for nonexempt staff I designed at VIVEX. This four-hour seminar not only put focus on the administrator but had a training component for the manager as well. The attendance was super, the evaluation feedback was stellar, and retention figures increased over a two-year period. I'm recapping this particular one because you spoke about the difficulty you're having holding on to top administrative talent, and I would hope I'd be able to set up and sell a similar career program to attack and eventually work to solve your problem."

Your OAR Story Answer

_____

_____

_____

_____

MISTAKES

Have you made any mistakes in your career? If so, what were they and how did you fix them?

Tip: This is an opportunity to test your honesty and your goals.

Sample OAR Story Answer

"'Mistake' may be too strong a word for any adjustments in my work, because I have tried to live my life fairly regret-free. Nevertheless, as I look back, I think I stayed at AGORIA about 18 months longer than necessary. I felt a strong sense of loyalty, though I was bored and ready to do more meaningful work. My boss was a young Turk and wasn't going anywhere either, not due to move up and not ready to move on. So, I learned a lesson about being proactive for my own career progress and am now much more suited to positive change."

Your OAR Story Answer

_____

_____

_____

_____

HANDLING OBJECTIONS, OVERCOMING RESISTANCE, AND RESOLVING SKEPTICISM

Most professional salespeople claim over-coming customer resistance is the toughest part of their job. A large segment of sales training seminars is spent rehearsing selling techniques: clarify the objection, resistance, or skepticism; provide relevant proof; overcome with benefits; and probe for acceptance.

In the context of a job interview, it may be difficult to do these steps. The key here is to respond without being defensive. Take whatever objection or concern that surfaces in the most open-minded way. Stay relaxed, try not to sit up straight abruptly or cross your hands in a flight-or-fight stance, and acknowledge the statement: "I can see how you'd think that" or "I would probably feel the same way if I were you." Then, address the objection, resistance, or skepticism directly for clarification, sell your benefits, and get acceptance.

> **HITS** (Hints, Insights, and Thoughts)
>
> Enroll in a professional sales course early in the search process. (Anyone who works can benefit. It should really be required for everyone's development plan.) You will learn a lifelong set of valuable skills, especially how to deal with difficult people and how to turn a negative response (or firmly stated objection) into a positive close. Most training uses a rehearsal methodology and videotape feedback that can make a huge difference in your learning.

Some interviewers throw in an objection just to see how you handle it. This is especially true for sales, marketing, or customer service job openings, but most likely the interviewer's legitimate concern stems from the thought that you might not be able to succeed at the job.

The question of a job candidate's overqualification surfaces a lot, especially in a tight job market. The interviewer may see you as overpriced (the compensation would never meet your expectations), overeager/desperate (the minute a better offer comes in, you'll leave); overskilled (the job isn't challenging enough to retain your interest), overexperienced (you have more working knowledge than the staff or the interviewer and may be difficult to manage), or just over the top (your fit seems too good to be true).

Remember never to mention money, and try to focus on what you can still learn and how you can make your boss or your team look good with your contributions. Sometimes the interviewer just has a bias, and that's a tough one to work out.

Sample OAR Story Answer

"I was pretty sure you would get to that issue eventually. Indeed, when I was hiring top talent, I was always on the alert for the consequences of bringing someone on board who had exceptional experience. In my case, I am still motivated by what I can learn (at GoGo I picked up on three new programs) and really believe all these working years make me a proven plug-and-play job performer—I can make a difference from the get-go. At SPRING, I improved sales revenue 15 percent over my first three months on the job.) Besides, I tend to create my own challenges and excitement (GoGo's shipping costs were reduced by 20 percent when I found a more efficient packing system.)

In response to the interviewer identifying you as underqualified, you need to ask "In what way?" (a clarifying attempt) and then try to respond directly to the objection that has surfaced.

Some objections raised, for example, "I don't think you have the right educational background," are vague and offered as an excuse not to hire you. Again, do your best to clarify: "What about my educational background concerns you?" or "Tell me, please, where my education falls short in meeting your needs?" Proceed to provide proof, sell benefits, and probe for acceptance.

Sample OAR Story Answer

"That may not be an issue, though I can certainly see your concern and reason for surfacing it. At HEEHAH—a business known only to hire top-tier school MBAs in its finance group—I was put in charge of revamping all of the accounting systems and procedures. My recommendations brought in about $100,000 in savings and were implemented on time and within budget. I got lots of accolades from the work group, and that meant much, too. I trust that resolves your initial concern about my credibility and working with your management hierarchy."

PTOS (Practical Tips and Opinions)

If you talk to a professional athlete or an actor or any performer, (s)he will almost always acknowledge getting nervous. When you are faced with a challenging situation, it's not only a natural, physiological response but also a positive source of energy, an opportunity to produce adrenaline that can be a source of enthusiasm and excitement. Getting nervous need not always be negative.

There are things you can do to control your nerves. Experiment with various techniques. Success depends on your own personal style, but practicing a few should help:

- *Prepare.* You will feel more in control if you have some idea of what you will say and how you will say it.

- *Practice.* You will feel more confident the more often you rehearse.

- *Release tension beforehand.* Take deep breaths. Hold your breath for a few seconds and exhale slowly, pressing your hands together, rolling or stretching your neck, and exercising the day before or morning of your interview. Ask for a glass of water if your mouth gets dry and keep your hands from shaking by holding them from view and making a fist for a second or two and then relaxing.

※ *Summary* ※

※ Thinking about your answers to the most common or overtly tricky questions will help.

※ Handling resistance is a sophisticated skill enhanced by a general nondefensive posture.

※ Getting nervous can be a good thing—managing to control it can be even better.

QUESTIONS YOU SHOULD ASK

Your asking questions is a key component of the interview and hiring process. Questions are another vital part of your data collection and, therefore, need to be well crafted and well thought-out so the answers can help you make an informed accept/not accept decision. In the end, you are in control and have the ultimate choice. You can always say "no" and pass on the offered opportunity if the answers you receive are unacceptable.

It's your responsibility, then, to do a thorough due diligence before making a decision—on the position, on the boss, and on the organization. Your questions also give you another chance to balance your sociability and competency levels and to impress the interviewer even more.

Good questions, in turn, also help your interviewer. They are additional tools for evaluation. An effective interviewer puts significance on what you ask almost as much as what you answer by seeing if this is the most desirable job or best fit. Your questions tell him/her a lot: how you think, what's important to you, and how well you gather data and assimilate it.

Because these questions are another form of the assessment process, you needn't be naïve about this side of the conversation. Certain questions you ask will put you in a poor first light: pushing too hard too early for details about promotions, benefits, vacation, job security, etc. Certain questions you don't ask might show you as not interested, or not politically astute or business savvy. Certain interviewers might also be threatened by some questions that by their nature might seem sophisticated and high powered and present you as arrogant vs. thoughtful.

Use the list of recommended questions here or create your own relevant set. Pick the ones that suit you and your style, and rewrite them if appropriate. The order *is* important. It helps show you as both strategic and tactical in your approach to the position.

Remember that writing good questions is a skill and requires some thought, as well. There are basically three different types of questions that will help you.

1. *The open-ended question.* This question encourages a free-form reply and gets the person talking. It's difficult to give a one-word answer when you use this question. Typically, it starts with What, Where, Why, When, or How.

2. *The mid/moderate-focus question.* This question enables you to dig deeper into the content and to gather data that might not surface in the very beginning. It not only can surface important facts but can also lengthen the time of your discussion. Typically, it starts with Explain, Tell me more, or Elaborate.

3. *The closed-ended question.* This question limits a reply to a one-word, yes-or-no answer, to some choice of alternatives you present, and to a single

number-related fact. It can shut down the dialogue and help you move the conversation forward faster. Typically, it starts with Can you, Are you, Would you, or Is it?

Because you are gathering data and do not want to prime for an answer or lead the witness, the open-ended or the mid/moderate-focused questions are generally best.

BUSINESS/COMPANY/INDUSTRY TRENDS

You need to know how the company is really doing and how it approaches its market, etc. Starting off with these questions

> **HITS** (Hints, Insights, and Thoughts)
>
> There is a tendency if things are going well in the interview to ask questions that will give you what you want to hear. This can be risky even in a noninterview setting and is no less risky in an interview. The leading question is its most common form, that is, the question that by construction is closed, trying to force an answer you want to hear or a perception you want validated. "You do provide a good benefit package, don't you?" or "Fridays are your fun days, right?" Try to avoid them. ("You like my new tie, don't you?" doesn't work either.)

positions you as a businessperson first, as someone who looks at the big picture and sees how everything fits. If you are meeting with a team of people, asking these kinds of questions will also help you test for consistency and overall vision. Whether you are meeting with HR, your direct manager, or even the CEO, they should bring valuable data. For example, if you are a low to moderate risk taker, discovering the organization of interest is not doing very well or is ripe for a takeover can certainly color your acceptance decision.

Shy away from asking any questions related to any pending lawsuits or negative publicity. You do not want to be seen as a potential troublemaker yourself. Save those questions for when you are onboard or have built a deeper relationship. Or, if you are working with an executive search organization and feel you must know, ask your representative recruiter his/her opinion.

- How is your company reacting to X trend? (Be sure to do research on the company and industry prior to the interview.)
- How is the company (budgets, etc.) affected by the state of the economy?
- What has the company done to strengthen itself in the prevailing economy?
- How is outsourcing overseas expected to impact the company?

- My research tells me that Company X is one of your major competitors. Do you agree, and whom else do you see as your major competitors?
- What differentiates you from the competition?
- What is a major company problem that you have yet to answer?
- Tell me your major challenges. What causes you greatest concern?
- What is the source of your company's name?
- What are the driving factors that protect your market share?
- What product or service do you think has the best potential to grow the business?
- Give me a view of the structure of your company.
- What are the business challenges for the next year?
- Where do you see your company's progress over the next five years?
- Tell me where your company stands against the trend toward _____.
- What is the biggest challenge XXX faces today?
- Where is the industry going and how will your company fare?

BOSS

Knowing as much about your boss as you can is also good business. You need to test for style compatibility and values and try to validate what you have observed in the interview or picked up from your other sources. (Build on the nonverbals—gesturing, nervous smiling, eye contact, etc.—as well as speech patterns, pacing, and balance of dialogue. Did (s)he speak especially rapidly and do all the talking, and other clues?)

Shy away from asking any personal questions (politics, for example) even though there might be an opportunity to do so (a casual down moment or something related to data you shared.) Save these topics for later on, if at all, and do what you can do minimize any red flags that might appear and avoid pushing a button.

- What work do you see yourself doing in five years?
- How do you reward employees that do well?
- How do you like to communicate with your employees?
- How is your success measured here?
- What kind of person do you work with best?
- Tell me about the confidence level in your department.

- How do you handle goal setting/objectives and track them?
- What would you do if your team was behind in a project? How would you motivate it?
- Tell me about your management style? (What do you like? Dislike?)
- What are the two areas here where you need the most help?
- Tell me about your relationship with your boss.
- How do new employees get management feedback?
- Tell me what a busy day looks like for you.
- Why do people like working for you?
- Who else is involved in making this hiring decision?
- What part of this company do you like or dislike?

> ### HITS (Hints, Insights, and Thoughts)
>
> Retention data confirms that the boss relationship is a key factor in your liking your work. No matter how terrific the organization is or how turned on you are by the work you are doing or accomplishing, a poor relationship with your boss can do you in.
>
> In some ways, it's like a romantic relationship, so follow your instincts. What you see is what you get. Rarely can you learn to "love" someone, when too many concerns surface. You cannot change your boss, no matter what you might think. Remember as well that this is not a partnership of equals. Your boss is in a power position. Weigh the data carefully. That same boss could also be gone in a month, and you with him/her.

- What would your staff tell me about you?
- What are your goals for this department?
- How do you grow employee competencies and educate staff? (Listen for mentoring options here.)
- Tell me about employees in your department who have done well and how they have progressed.
- Tell me about position advancement in your department.

A subset of the boss questions are those directly related to your position, those questions that are not fully explained in the job description, might need additional clarification, and/or did not get answered during the main portion of the interview. Some of these questions, of course, might be better positioned in the second interview or at your first-day meeting.

Shy away, right now, from questions that might indicate your interest in other, nonjob benefits, asking for special consideration or a promotion too early, or signaling an unwillingness to perform a requirement: "What are my chances of writing the movie reviews?" "When can I begin to telecommute?" "How much keyboard work is really involved?" "When are you eligible for an internal transfer?"

Job/position questions could be:

- What are the hours of the graveyard shift here?
- How will I know I am meeting the external customer requirements?
- How much time is typically involved in _____?
- What is the company's executive travel policy?

STAFF/DEPARTMENT

Your co-workers and the relationships you have with them are often seen as another determinant of job satisfaction. Indeed, it cannot influence your enjoyment of the job itself or the rewards received from it, but if the associations are not positive or at least cordial, it can certainly damage you and make you not want to go to work in the morning. The interviewer should be testing for a smooth fit: Will the team embrace you? Will you get along with everyone? Will you bring the one skill that is a bit light now? You should do the same. Shy away from questions that might indicate you have a problem in getting along with others or are overly aggressive and not instinctively a team player.

- Why is this job available? Is it newly created or did the one in this role leave?
- What are the skills and experience level of the staff?
- Tell me about the team dynamics.
- How long have the most senior and junior persons been with the company?
- How is your department viewed in this organization?
- How big is your group as a percentage of the company workforce?
- What are some of the team development activities in the department?
- What are some of the results of the work done?
- Who internally (if anyone) has applied for this position?
- What are the immediate deliverables for this group?
- What is the reporting structure?
- What is the predominant means of communication?

- How do you measure success for individuals, staff, and the organization?
- How much does the political organizational chart agree with the administrative organizational chart?
- What is the communication like within the group?
- How well does your group's skill set contribute to the company's objectives?
- How do you see this position relating to various internal teams?

ENVIRONMENT/CULTURE

No one wants to work in a place that isn't fun, isn't giving back to the community, isn't customer driven, isn't receptive to working couples, isn't quality-minded or isn't . . . whatever. Also, certain personality types do better at certain companies. Of course, it's hard to assess the culture or the personality of an organization, but your questions will help you distinguish and find a fit. So will your network.

In some ways, it's like finding the right college. Some places also have distinct reputations: combative, free form/loose, or even sweatshop-like. Try your best to ferret out the reality.

Shy away from asking directly about the culture. This is one of those questions ("What is the culture like here?") that encourages canned answers or a pre-planned response that interviewers are often trained to give—a politically correct answer or what the person thinks you want to hear.

- What do people like about working here?
- What do people dislike about working here?
- How do you celebrate successes at your company?
- Your company's vision statement says "you're flexible" and "you're customer-focused." How are these qualities fulfilled by your group?
- How do people here handle difficult circumstances?
- Give me an example of your group structure. What systems are in place?
- What's the typical turnover per year in the organization?
- What do people do for fun here?
- How often does the team get together after work?
- How important is a college degree here?

- What's the team spirit like here on a Friday afternoon?
- How does teamwork show itself?
- What is the office dress code?
- How would you describe a week's workload and how would your staff describe it?
- What work ethics (values) exist here?
- How open is management about sharing employee ideas/information?
- How much input do employees have to influence the company culture?

SELF

If you ask you shall receive. Despite the legal risk of saying something off mark, most interviewers will try to give you some indication of how you look to them or how you compare to your competition—if you ask. Feedback during the interview is especially important. It can turn around a perception, dispel a bias, or even eliminate an objection. Asking questions about where you stand can also put you in a positive position with your interviewer. It illustrates your eagerness to accept feedback and your willingness to act on it.

Shy away from questions that might put your interviewer on the spot or make him/her uncomfortable or uneasy. Give him/her some kind of out if at all possible, and be mindful that the person may not be as candid and forthcoming as you would want and a canned answer might surface here, as well.

- Are there any obstacles I would need to overcome to succeed in this job?
- What opportunities for growth exist in this position?
- Given my background, are there any concerns you have about my ability to succeed in this position?
- What additional tasks are part of the position that do not appear in the job description?
- How does my background in X or Y fit your needs?
- How do I compare to the ideal candidate and which of my skills match this best?
- What do you need to know about me that will assure you I can do this job?
- Tell me what your non-negotiable, must-haves are for this position.
- What credentials inspired you to grant me this interview? Given what you've learned so far, what do you see as my greatest strength and why?

- What in my qualifications concerns you?
- How do I compare with the previous person who held the job?
- I've always been interested in_____; how can the company help me to stay current?
- What are the critical success factors for this position?
- What are the training opportunities for new employees?
- What is your experience with assigning mentors, and who would that be?
- If I'm hired, what would you expect me to achieve in the next three to six months? In the first year?

FUTURE PLANS/NEXT STEPS

Finally, you should pose some questions that will help you move forward. It's important you ask about the timing of what you should do next, so you can "go for the close." It's also best if you get permission to call for a status report so you are not kept waiting if the interviewer gets busy and postpones the call back. Waiting is very anxiety producing; you can help minimize it with some kind of time frame.

A fast return call or an immediate request to come back is a good sign. Very often, a long wait or a not-so-fast reply means that someone else is the top candidate. Sometimes you are number two and are kept waiting until number one makes the decision. Hang in there.

Shy away from any question that can put the interviewer on the defensive. You are letting the person know you want the job and are willing to play by the rules. You just need to know what they are.

- When would you want the hire to be on the job and productive?
- When do you expect to make a hiring decision?
- When can I expect to hear feedback from you?
- If I don't hear from you by X, may I call you by Y?
- Who else is involved in this hiring decision? How can I convince them I am right for the job?
- Is there anything else you need from me at this point?
- Where are you in this hiring process? How many other candidates are you considering?
- How many people have you interviewed?

- How many candidates will be called back for a second interview?
- What is your process of candidate selection?
- What is the percentage of my chance to be hired?
- What is the next step in filling this position? How do you want me to interact during the interview process?
- How long has this position remained open?
- What aspects about the organization should I consider prior to the next interview?

PTOS (Practical Tips and Opinions)

If some of the answers you receive raise red flags of concern for you, try to remain open-minded at this point and concentrate on continuing to sell your strong points. Play it out until an offer comes, and try not to rule out the position even if something surfaces that you see as a deal breaker. Get asked to the prom so you have the choice to say no.

Very often there isn't enough interview time to get the questions you need and want answered. It's certainly acceptable and within range to ask the interviewer what to do or how to resolve some of the unanswered questions that are important to you. Take your cues from him/her and follow up with the recommendation provided. (Perhaps e-mailing a set of questions that are important to you.)

Remember to select questions that suit your audience and be mindful that there is a risk that something asked could trigger a politically sensitive hot button, could backfire, or could telegraph a personal sophistication level that could be threatening or damaging. Carefully select the questions that reflect you best and think before you move.

✳ *Summary* ✳

✳ Knowing the three types of questions—open-ended, mid/moderate-focus, and closed—should help you create a mix that keeps the interviewer's interest and helps you discover the facts.

✳ Practicing your questions beforehand will help with tone, inflection, pace, etc. These are areas that could create some negativity.

✳ Keeping an open mind at this point—despite negative signals—keeps you in control when an offer comes. You can always refuse.

✳ Asking thought-provoking and powerful questions has its risks. Be aware, and choose those that fit your audience and present you as thoughtful vs. arrogant.

VARIATIONS ON THE INTERVIEW THEME

Interviews take many shapes and forms, from the expected one-on-one discussed in the previous chapters to the impromptu discussion at a dinner party or soccer match. You need to be aware of the various formats so you can be as prepared as possible. Each requires a slightly different approach and a slightly different set of expectations.

> **HITS** (Hints, Insights, and Thoughts)
>
> Knowing the motivation behind the question asked and how it relates to the specific position will help you craft the appropriate answer. For example, a salesperson needs to deal with rejection, so a question about handling disappointment might include something about your knowing when to move on from an unreasonable deal or your ability to rebound once you have analyzed what might have gone wrong or even what you can learn from the encounter. The same might apply for how you handle an objection or resistance. Always assume there is a logical reason for everything you are asked.

TRADITIONAL ONE-ON-ONE

The one-on-one interview is perhaps the most common version you can experience. It's typically prescheduled and takes place in the interviewer's office or the company conference room. It requires a relaxed, conversational approach (similar to a business meeting—not a martial-arts encounter) for you to be successful. Sometimes the setting is a restaurant, coffeehouse, or an airline executive lounge. It's important to avoid eating or drinking anything that will impede your ease of conversation or distract from your sales pitch: avoid pizza, spaghetti, or thick drinks that require a straw or spoon.

Search out the quietest spot possible (a corner table maybe), if you are in a public place, and be mindful of the volume of your voice. Nothing is more annoying than to have the person next to you nodding or adding points to your questions or answers. Take your ordering cues from the interviewer, but be sure to carry enough money with you to treat, even though the interviewer will most likely offer to pay. The tips and recommendations in previous chapters show the best approaches for your success. Those people most likely to conduct your traditional one-on-ones are the HR professional, your hiring manager, and your co-workers.

The Human Resource Interview

The human resource interview searches for the proper corporate, executive, or cultural fit and is often conducted by a trained HR professional seeking the right look, level of confidence, ease of conversation, or balance of drive and motivation. (Some larger organizations hire outside firms to do prehire assessment for the most senior staff). If the corporate systems are in place and functioning well, the HR interview will come first. Even if you enter with a recommendation from the CEO and are successful in the interviews that follow, you will need to meet someone in the HR group before an offer is made. The human resource interview can make or break you, no matter who is championing your cause.

The Hiring Manager Interview

The hiring manager interview is done by the would-be boss and emphasizes the job's specific tasks and the candidate's role on his/her team or department. It's a nuts-and-bolts interview, full of detailed questions about real job scenarios: what you can do and how you would do it. Though many organizations now provide their managers with sophisticated how-to interview training seminars (with much emphasis on the legal do's and don'ts—see Chapter 5 for more details), the hiring manager is often solely focused on getting the work accomplished. (Think of any time you have hired someone to do involved tasks for you: You wanted to be sure that even the kid you chose to shovel your snow could get the job done, or else you may not have gotten out of the driveway to go to work.)

> **HITS** (Hints, Insights, and Thoughts)
>
> If you are fortunate enough to interview in the person's office, you will learn something that might not be as discernable in a conference room or public setting. For example, attractive artwork and interesting decorator artifacts might signal a dramatic flair or an interest in travel or the arts. Books and manuals might signal an intellectual bent or a special interest in personal learning and professional development. Posted diplomas tell you something, as does children's art or lots of family photographs. Use these "signs" to help you connect to your customer.

The Co-Worker Interview

The co-worker interview tests and evaluates to see if the interviewer likes you and sees you working compatibly, comfortably, and productively in his/her department or work group. (S)he may not have much interview training but is certainly able to sense an arrogant tone or too casual behavior. In this case, be competent yet nonthreatening, and be brief about your background statements, answers, and questions. Your goal is to be seen as a collaborative, easy-to-work-with team player, not as a know-it-all superstar who is supercompetitive and threatening to even the most competent employee.

INTERVIEW APPROACHES

The various one-on-one interviews come in different formats. Knowing the various combinations and understanding the approaches in your exchange can tell you something about the interviewer and the organization.

Structured Interview

The structured interview typically allows you about 65 percent and the interviewer 35 percent of the talk time. Questions, prepared and scripted in advance, are adapted to meet the specific criteria of the position, and they are used to determine your competencies in meeting the job responsibilities. There is a time limit and a logical flow to the process. Watch the interviewer, as (s)he may also be taking notes on your replies to the questions while you are speaking. Remember not to embellish thoughts or ask questions if you see the interviewer jotting thoughts (or circling ranking numbers on a structured list of questions). These notes may be crucial—especially if they're positive marks—to the hiring process. They may be gathered later and studied to distinguish your responses from many other competitors' comments.

Unstructured Interview

The unstructured interview is not the opposite of a structured interview. The goals are the same, but the process is much less formal. More conversational and open in tone and approach, here the interviewer asks questions that get you talking—hopefully not rambling. A skillful interviewer using this "just talk between pals" technique can get you to let down your professional guard and blab negatives about former work. The interviewer probes deep into the replies to discover and raise red-flag issues. Some applicants see the unstructured interview as a poker game with bluffs or aces up one's sleeve. But if you regard the proceedings as a competition with the interviewer, you'll be the one folding your cards in the job game.

Behavioral Interview

The behavioral interview looks to your past experiences as indicators of your future success on the job. Interviewers prepare questions that test what you have done and how you have succeeded with what the position requires. A typical behavioral question begins as, "Tell me about a time when you" or "How did you deal with any employee whose performance was below your standards." Your responses need to tell the interviewer how you approach your work, how you apply your skills and talents, and how you deal with work issues and problems.

Free-Form Interview

A free-form interview is filled with questions that seem unrelated and unfocused. Random and unpredictable, it often reflects the interviewer's lack of experience rather than a strategy or purposeful approach to garnering candidate information. Quite often the interviewer does not take notes and does most of the talking.

With this freewheeling dialogue, your goal is to connect positively right away and to work stories and experiences into the conversation that highlight your accomplishments. Smile a lot, be warm and natural, nod when you acknowledge your empathy, and cite your success stories as examples that identify with similar circumstances expressed by your interviewer.

HITS (Hints, Insights, and Thoughts)

Remember information and preparation are the two key words for a successful interview. The more you *know*—from the best route there to the dress code, type of interview, environment, etc.—and the more you can *practice*—from a sample phone screening to a mock videotaping, etc.—the greater your real-time success will be. Leave as little to chance as possible, *never arrive late, never eat or chew anything*, and assume the interview will be conducted by a professional who has also prepared and trained for your being there.

The Casual One-on-One

This interview is a more spontaneous experience, one you might not even expect, at a place you might not think official or even appropriate. "We are always selling" is the adage of choice here. The person you meet at a meeting or a sporting event can certainly ask a few of the questions you will encounter formally: "Tell me about yourself" or "What are you most proud of?" or "What would people say if I called and asked?"

Be sure you are prepared. Have a copy of your resume to present and try not to look too surprised and flustered. (Yes, you should never leave the house in too grungy a state when you are in search mode, and you should have the latest version of your resume, your business card, and a pen and paper to record your person's contact particulars *always nearby* (bike basket, glove compartment, wife's purse, husband's sports bag, etc.) Have a mental miniscript of at least the five or six questions that always come up for you.

Be mindful of the time situation and what might be going on around you. (You'd hate to miss your daughter's one goal of the year!) Crisper than normal answers would be best here. Close each query with an assumptive sales line such as, "I can provide additional details here or an extended version, when we meet more formally in your office." Your goal is to continue the encounter.

Even these off-the-cuff interviews require some follow-up. An e-mail request for continuation or a voice mail thanks are in order. Be careful that you take the person's name down correctly if (s)he does not have a business card ready. Misspellings hurt you in any situation. People are not that forgiving, even if the interview process began at your sister-in-law's baby shower.

GROUP INTERVIEW

The group or panel interview has several people in a room asking questions at the same time. This examination can be overwhelming, especially if you aren't expecting it. Make sure you know in advance if this approach is part of the interview. You don't want to find out only when you enter the interview room that there are five people seated on one side of a conference table and you on the other. You may feel you're before a congressional hearing.

Answering questions coming from many people's perspectives is difficult to master. Just remember that only one person can ask you a question at a time. Try to look directly at the person when answering his/her question, then "visit" the others in the room, scanning the group and glancing at each person to check for his acknowledgement or understanding (his "buy in"). Try to remember each person's name, and be sure you close with a statement of your interest in the job, too.

Be sure to maintain sure eye contact and balance your responses to all inter-viewers (ignoring or isolating even one interviewer may lead to that person blackballing you). It's sort of like handing your "treats" out to most but not all takers and then getting a "trick" from an empty-handed, disgruntled person.

Take your cue from your audience. If the room is a large one with poor acoustics or if you're continually asked to repeat the question, make an attempt to paraphrase or restate what's been asked. Use the person's name, too, if you remember it: "So, Rocky's interested in my greatest professional accomplish-ment in the last four years. Well . . ."

Be careful not to fiddle with your hands, tap your feet, polish your shoes on your pants, pull down your skirt or jacket, or move around too much. Even though you may be at a table, each interviewer there sees you from a little different angle, and you are much more exposed than when in a one-on-one.

SIMULATION INTERVIEW

Sometimes you are encouraged to participate with other candidates in a pre-planned activity. The experiential exercise or simulation interview can also be a part of a corporate-sponsored assessment center to predict success in groups. You and other applicants work together on a simulated group project, observed by the trained evaluating staff. (The concept is similar to Donald Trump's approach made famous on TV's *The Apprentice*).

Your performance here is another measure of potential success on the job. Follow directions carefully and participate warmly, knowing your ability to solve problems, take a leadership role, and/or collaborate are key success indicators. Remember not to be too bossy or boisterous (or too assertive for that matter). There is a fine line between demonstrating skills and swamping the competition in a way that shows you're not a team player.

SERIAL INTERVIEW

The round robin or serial interview is when you are moved from one interviewer to another. In this case, you get to meet and talk with your potential co-workers, employees, and other organizational team members—you know, those you will join in the office sports or lottery pools. It requires a combination of energy, patience, and enthusiasm for you to be successful here. Sometimes there can be as many as six interviews in one day, often with you conducting a slide presentation or stand-up delivery as well!

Be sure your serial interview answers are consistent (often group members meet to critique and assess your replies), and your tone is pleasantly upbeat, not fatigued from repetition. Indeed, you may be drained, but you should not express boredom or exhaustion. Rather, if you must cite similar statements to one interviewer after another, use the repetition to further fortify your story or even add effective new selling points that will occur to you the longer you proceed and the more comfortable you become talking about your value to others.

Be prepared for someone who might want to test your skills at assessing personalities and could use these questions as a casual opener: "You're among the lucky applicants who had a chance to spend some time with P.J., whadya think of her?" Remember you are there to sell yourself and your fit for the position, group or organization, *not* to get involved in department or corporate politics, take sides, or pass judgment. Your answer needs to be honest, something like, "It's really hard just after 35 minutes or so, but she seemed just fine to me." No need for pop psychology here despite what the situation might really be.

Be sure you have an energy bar available or can get some chocolate or a caffinated drink. The person interviewing you in late afternoon should see the same energy level as the person you meet first thing in the morning.

TELEPHONE/SCREENING INTERVIEW

Another interview variation, a subset of the one-on-one, is the screening or telephone interview in which a trained person or HR staff representative tests for specific requirements, such as certification musts—exposure to certain tools, etc.—and eliminates noncontenders from a large pool of candidates. Telephone screening interviews are used when the volume of responses is huge and asking each potentially suitable candidate to the office is impractical and expensive.

Your response on the phone can make the difference in your moving forward in the process and getting a call for an in-person meeting. Here are a few general tips, some that even the telemarketing professionals find helpful:

- *Stand up when talking on the phone.* This posture can open your diaphragm and produce a clear, well-projected voice.
- *Smile.* You'll feel more relaxed, and your listener will hear that confident tone in your voice.
- *Move about if you are able and have a portable phone.* This activity can generate and increase your positive energy level.
- *Keep a copy of your resume handy.* Put it near your phone (along with the coffee, of course) for easy reference, and make sure your accomplishments are highlighted for quick facts at your fingertips.
- *Answer "yes" first to any closed question, and then clarify and explain afterwards, if necessary.* Know that most screeners are working from a checklist of prepared questions—often directly related to a desired skill or special requirement. The person is most likely to check the yes box, if the word comes up consistently, or if he remembers your instinctive reply.

- *Reserve quiet time and place if possible for this conversation, especially if you initiate the return call.* Try to maintain a professional perspective; in other words, turn down the game on your desk radio and close your door to your kids or pets shuffling through the house.

- *Take the call vs. returning it.* It's difficult to get back to a recruiter or screener who is bent on completing what could be a long list of names to contact, even if you are in a strange place on your cell phone and can arrange a mutually agreed call-back time. Move to that quiet place or at least put the caller on hold, so you can get to one, catch your breath, gain your composure, and set your mind to selling your features and benefits.

THE VIDEO INTERVIEW/CONFERENCE

Sometimes an interested organization wants to meet you right away but schedules and finances make that impossible. This is true especially if you are not within commuting distance from the future employer. The video interview is an increasingly popular option. It can be a one-on-one experience or a panel or group encounter. Sometimes, if there is a corporate satellite office near you, you are invited there and have the interview in a company space with its equipment. Other times, you will need to go to a public facility, such as FedEx Kinko's, where the company arranges to rent space and video equipment for you. In either situation, all of the advice presented for the one-on-one or group interview will help you on video, too.

Try not to worry about the camera. Once you begin talking, it's easier to forget about it. Besides if you did that recommended mock-interview practice, you are already primed and more comfortable in front of the lens, though it *is* different when there isn't anybody in the room with you. In any case, visit a facility that has video teleconferencing capability. It should help ease your possible real time stress if you know in advance what to expect. Space layout and equipment may vary, but you will at least get some idea of the drill.

Take the camera's limitations into account. Wear a light blue or an off-white blouse/shirt and avoid huge stripes or vibrant colors. The camera responds better to softer tones and less pattern activity. (No black-eyed make-up either.)

Give good eye contact to the person talking to you—look directly at the TV—and reply appropriately with smiles, nods, and other normal good-listening reactions. Try to downplay your gestures. Even the slightest eye roll or puzzled smirk looks overblown and over obvious on camera. Stage actors need to relearn reactions when a TV gig comes along.

Wait and be sure the question or thought is complete before crafting your answer or reply. There is often a slight delay with even the most expensive and sophisticated equipment, and you do not want to interrupt or step on the person's words. The extra second here trumps the rapid-fire response. Also, bring a paper and pencil to the session so you can immediately jot down names and sitting positions of those interviewing you. You can glance at this "seating chart" later on if you need help remembering a name to use during the meeting.

INTERVIEW CONVENTIONS

Except for an on-the-go, off-the-cuff, or super spontaneous encounter, there are certain format conventions and rules of give and take between interviewer and applicant that surface in each variation of the job interview.

- The interviewer should have your resume and/or application and some idea of what to ask you. You should bring extra copies just in case and have prior knowledge of the company, the interviewer, or the position.
- The interviewer will try to welcome you graciously and attempt to establish a relaxed atmosphere, initiating small talk about directions or offering you something to eat or drink. This person may personally introduce you to everyone you will talk to.
- You should smile and repeat the name of everyone you meet initially, including the receptionist. Maybe one day soon you will be working with these people. You should also greet everyone with a professional handshake and be sociable, at ease, and forthcoming.
- The interviewer poses the questions; you provide the answers. When the interviewer asks for questions, you then pose issues that are important to you (other than salary terms, which will most likely be raised only after you have been selected as the preferred candidate).
- The interviewer closes the discussion, sells the job and organization if appropriate, and sets the next-steps discussion. Never close the inter-

view at your convenience, or you will have closed the door on your chances.

- You thank everyone for their time—verbally at the time and with a note afterwards—get follow-up agreements, shake hands, and part company.

THE INFORMATION-ONLY INTERVIEW

Meeting new people and learning about what's going on in your industry or profession provides you with important data you can use to your advantage in the future (see Chapter 4 in my other book *Hire Me, Inc.*). Remember that you position this meeting as not wanting a job but instead as wanting an introduction to a "player," to learn something new, or to meet others "in the know" who might also help. You want to learn as much as you can.

You should see the information interview as a key component of your networking strategy. In many ways, it can be the most valuable part of your overall search process and can lead to that official job interview and that closed sale. Attending a professional association meeting, asking your friends and family for names, and keeping your eyes and ears open at all times are a few ways you can begin to meet people to interview.

Here, too, arrive on time and relaxed, comfortable with your objectives and accomplishments to date. Be gracious about your contact's needs, but stay focused on your objectives. Take care to use the allotted time wisely. Leave both your business card and a copy of your resume. Follow up with a thank-you note. (See Figure 8.1.) And deliver on anything you promised to do because you should perform professionally in the information interview process as if it were already your first day on a new job—without asking for the paycheck, of course. It's important that you do not come on too strong or push too much. You are soft selling and collecting research vs. "pounding the pavement" or "dialing for dollars," trying to make your end-of-the month sales quota. Be sure to have some sample questions to ask your contact to assure your networking success. And be sure to take the Post-Interview Assessment in Figure 8.2.

Figure 8.1: Sample Thank-You Letter (or E-Mail) for Your Information Interview

August 20, 200X

Mr. Billy Bob Wharton
Director, Okawalla Beverages
3 Indian Lane
Half Moon Bay, CA 54578

Dear Mr. Wharton:

Yesterday morning's meeting was an especially productive one for me. Thank you. I appreciate your finding time in your busy schedule to talk to me. I am already following your suggestions to contact more trade officials, including Henry Wackler and Doris Weeks at Pepsi.

I have a meeting with Doris next week and have calls already into the DNA.

Again thanks for all your help. I'll keep you posted on my progress.

Regards,

J.D. Drink

J.D. Drink

P.S. My Mom sends her special best.

Figure 8.2: **Post-Interview Assessment**

It's important at the end of any key interview to assess how it went. You will continue to learn from each interview experience you have and the assessment sheet that follows will help you continue to improve.

What did you do to connect positively with your interviewer? _____

_____

What technical questions were asked? _____

_____

Which ones were the most difficult for you to answer? Why? _____

_____

What questions did you answer successfully? _____

_____

What questions caused you to stumble or you did not think went well? Why? _____

_____

What questions did you ask? _____

_____

What questions are still unanswered? _____

_____

How would you rate your success in the interview on a scale of 1 to 5 (1 = missed the mark; 5 = nailed it)? _____

_____

What will you include in your thank you that will help solidify the deal or repair what you might have missed? _____

_____

Figure 8.2: **Post-Interview Assessment,** continued

What have you learned from this experience? _____

_____

What will you do differently next time? _____

_____

SAMPLE INFORMATION INTERVIEW QUESTIONS

Here again the questions you ask tell a lot about you and how your personality or style might fit the organization or mesh well with the person you are meeting. Think carefully about which questions suit you and feel free to craft the query in a way that's most comfortable for you.

Information/Data

The facts you collect here will help you learn invaluable information about the industry, both past, present, and future, and something about your contact at the company, as well. If you are looking to change fields or enter a new arena, you will be able to assess how the data compares or matches your perceptions or expectations, and your interests and skills.

Shy away from asking *directly* if there is a job for you and be sure not to shift the focus of your discussion to a real-time job interview. Be careful also not to ask for information that could be seen as too personal—lifestyle balance or family particulars. Your boundaries are professional ones, and your contact is there to help you, not to take you on.

- What are the best career development opportunities in this industry?
- Do the professionals in your field with the same job title have similar responsibilities or are there other job titles that have comparable scope of duties?
- What are the possibilities for jobs in this field now? Industry in general?

- What would it take to be hired by an organization with your kind of profile?
- What are the major industry trends?
- What are the best jobs?
- What individual personality traits are best suited for this kind of work?
- How would you characterize your work environment (e.g., structured or unstructured, work independently or with a team, seasonal peak time, etc.)
- Which professional publications and organizations do you consider relevant to this career field?

Ideas

Once more you are in data collection mode, with a goal of increasing your understanding and knowledge base. Shy away from asking questions that would assume you are an insider. Remember also not to imply in any way that you would use an idea inappropriately or for reasons other than to move you forward in your job/career search.

- What key information should I know about this field?
- What background do you usually require?
- What do you find most rewarding about your job?
- What do you find least rewarding?
- What reference material would be pertinent for me to read about this industry?
- What professional organizations recruit members in this industry?
- What are the possibilities in doing volunteer work?
- Since nothing is perfect, what are some of the pressures your group experiences?

HITS (Hints, Insights, and Thoughts)

Communication theorists agree that it is much more difficult to *receive* critical or improvement feedback than it is to deliver or present it. Below are some tips that should help you accept input that might not be easy to hear:

- Focus on what is being said vs. who is saying it.
- Listen calmly, openly, and attentively.
- Reaffirm the other person's reactions and issues.
- Refrain from defending or overexplaining.
- Solicit suggestions for improvement.

Advice

This line of questioning should be your easiest. Most people love giving advice and see your interest as a positive ego boost. Shy away from asking questions that make your contact uncomfortable or are too difficult to answer.

- What would you do if you were in my position?
- If you were in my position, which competitor would you interview with?
- What did you do to gain your present role?
- How did you break into the industry?
- What strikes you about my resume?
- Would you hire me?
- What advice do you have for someone preparing for this career?
- Major in school? Special courses?
- Advanced degree a must or just helpful?
- Any extracurricular activities you think could help?
- How can I spend my job-hunting time most effectively?
- To someone who knows you well enough: Given my experience, what is a key tip you have for me?

Feedback/Recommendations

Here again there should be no real issue. Most people have no problem giving feedback (especially the improvement or corrective kind) and telling you what to do. The resume is one of the best vehicles for that.

Shy away from questions that make your contact uneasy, and be sure you accept the feedback with a nondefensive thank you. "Yes . . . buts" are not a good policy any time you receive input, but especially in this situation when someone you might not know well is taking the time to pass on some wisdom.

Make sure you accept the input you get from your networking contact graciously. One Silicon Valley HR professional came to solicit advice and then proceeded to discount each recommendation given: "I can't do that because" or "I already tried that and" or "I don't like that method." She closed the meeting by asking for feedback on our time together. I took the risk, checking that she did indeed want some straight talk, and informed her she would have come off better by accepting the input less judgmentally, even if she chooses not to use it later on: "I didn't consider that approach. Thanks." or, "I'll look into that. Glad you mentioned it." Feedback is like a gift at holiday time. You thank the person when you get it and only return it after you acknowledge and appreciate the gesture. She took everything in and thanked me for my honesty. No one else had clued her in, and she realized that her approach might have alienated some of her network.

- Looking at my resume, how do you think I could make it better? Fit in as a _____?
- What is a key item you'd change on my resume?
- What suggestions do you have for me to enhance my chances (e.g., training, networking, promoting, etc.) to be a _____?
- What other questions might I ask to gain even more specific information about this industry's jobs?
- What value did you get from our time together?
- May I contact you in the future?

Names to Contact

You need names to move your networking forward. It never hurts to ask, but it does hurt if you badger the person. Some people are insular by nature and just do the job and do not get out and about much. Accept this, and leave if no names surface. Shy away from asking questions that refer to gossip or rumor or reputation of others. This, too, can backfire.

- Can you recommend others in your organization I may meet? (It's important to get additional new contact names as part of your current informational interview.)
- Who can I talk to for a broader perspective on the company? Or on the industry? May I use your name?
- My goal is three new people who might help—anyone you can think of in your world?

> **HITS** (Hints, Insights, and Thoughts)
>
> Your information interview should include a mix of those question types discussed in Chapter 7—open-ended, mid/moderate-focus, and closed. You know you've been successful if you gather data, ideas, advice, feedback/recommendations, and three names in a way that builds the self-esteem of your source and does not threaten, badger, or put her on the spot.

PTOS (Practical Tips and Opinions)

- Remember, a job interview is not an opportunity to let your hair down, unload your dirty laundry, or report your secret intimacies, even if the situation is especially comfortable and conversation is friendly and easy. Saying nothing can become an advantage stategy.

A senior HR professional was closing an interview by asking the candidate about her name Donin, which seemed unique to him. She responded that her father Donald and her mother Ina combined their names to create hers. "Very clever," he responded. "Nowadays no one would *ever* do that—much too hokey dokey for today's sophisticated world." Only after she was hired and on staff for a few months did he learn that she had only one child, a son named Jadin, a combination of his father Jack and his mother Donin!

He couldn't resist asking why she didn't say anything during the hiring interview. She chuckled and asserted that disclosing her son's name then might have positioned her as "hokey dokey" vs. the professional presence she spent creating during the bulk of the interview.

✳ *Summary* ✳

✳ Knowing the various kinds of interviews reinforces your requirement for preparation and practice.

✳ Coming on too strong and not weighing the risks of both your questions and answers can backfire. Answer and ask what's comfortable for you and at a time you think is best for the situation.

✳ Understanding yourself—your strengths and weaknesses, especially— is still the cornerstone for how you choose to handle various interview situations and questions that come up.

Close Down
and Next Steps

Even when you interview successfully, the process is not over—you cannot afford to let your guard down or to ease up on your professionalism or followthrough. How you handle post interview interactions is also a series of significant behaviors.

NEGOTIATING THE BEST DEAL

Once you have completed the required interviews and sent off your thank-you notes, you need to sit tight and wait until the agreed time of response. In years past, if you were kept waiting a long time and did not hear anything, it was not a positive signal. Nowadays, with checkerboard travel schedules and many minds helping to make the hiring decision, it could just mean a missed deadline or a reference that's been difficult to reach. It could also mean you are the number-two person, and the hiring manager is waiting for number one to make a move.

You might also be called back to meet more people. All tips and techniques apply here, as well. Even though someone may indicate "it's just a formality" or "Jane just wants to check you out," treat any return visit as very important and like any other interview you have. Remember not to let your guard down, imply that you're just waiting for the offer letter or the formal go-ahead, or become too casual and matter of fact. Being over-confident and cocky could ruin everything.

NO OFFER

Sometimes the offer does not come, despite positive signals from the interview process. If you are working with a recruiter, now is the time to get as much feedback as you can on what really happened. Sometimes the job was put on hold, other times an internal candidate was selected. There is also the possibility that your references didn't click or the final interviews were not as powerful as you thought. See if you can get some corrective input from the recruiter that could help you in the future.

If you did not use a recruiter, try to make contact with the hiring manager yourself to learn why you were not selected. Many employers are reluctant to pass on any substantive information—sometimes fearing a discrimination lawsuit—yet the feedback you can get will help you in the future. Comments like "You came off a bit cocky" or "You were a bit too aggressive with the VP" are behaviors that are readily modified for the next interview. Emphasize that you value the insight and can use suggestions to secure a similar position elsewhere.

Some professionals recommend that you follow up the rejection with a quick letter to the HR contact or the hiring manager, letting him/her know you were disappointed but hope to be considered for other work at the organization in the future. Leave the door open to fresh contact because sometimes if you call back in a few months, the selected candidate may have left and you can revive the company's interest in your skills.

It's most satisfying and very natural to want to take a bow when your offer arrives. Getting the job offer is an especially satisfying reward that comes from all of your hard work and careful strategy. It validates that the company sees value in your strengths and wants you to be a part of its organization. You should enjoy the thrill of making the sale.

> **HITS** (Hints, Insights, and Thoughts)
>
> The adage "It's not over 'til the fat lady sings" has a job search counterpart: "It's not over 'til you're at your desk on day 1." You need to be on your guard at all times. Too many jobs have been lost at the very last minute over a hang-tough, off-the wall negotiation request or at the elevator with an inappropriate throw-away line, politically incorrect joke, or foul language slip. Keep your most professional persona.

Nevertheless, your ultimate goal is the right job, not just any job. You must evaluate your offer in the context of your short- and long-term career aspirations. It is your choice. (Certainly, the number of offers—perhaps this is the only one so far—and the time you have been looking are practical and key issues to consider.)

Your nod is typically made over the phone first, which is not surprising. Most companies like to check in before creating and delivering the more formal offer letter and want to be sure you're still interested in the position. Avoid evaluating the job and your responsibilities or money and benefits negotiation until you have your offer letter in hand. Many deals have been lost at this I'm-preparing-an-offer-and-want-to-know-what-you-think stage. You don't want to create doubts where there were none or suggest lofty job expectations or personal needs that show you as a poor team player. Besides, you need to be sure you are getting everything you want—a letter can give you that specific assurance.

Here are some tasks to do when your letter does arrive:

- *Get some time.* Give yourself the opportunity to fully ponder the offer. It's OK to ask for the time. The extra few days can help you make the right decision and should not cause HR havoc at the organization. State your interest and appreciation in the proposal and explain that this consideration time reflects your business sincerity. (Suitable replies to the offer, if pressed, include, "I need to talk it over with my family" or "I am waiting for an offer from another company, and want to decide what's the best one for me." You can play this delaying tactic as a bluff, counting on the company to get nervous and sweeten its offer, but you also risk losing the genuine offer you have—so this is perhaps a ploy best left to poker players and frequent car buyers.)

- *Get some closure.* Be sure to call the other organizations interested in your candidacy and let them know you have an offer in hand and are eager to hear from them. Craft your words carefully, and ask for the status of the process. See if you can create a sense of urgency in moving forward, without threatening, bragging, or offending. You might say, "We agreed I'd let you know if another offer came through, and, well, one has, this morning. I was hoping you'd let me know how close you are to making a decision. I'm still very interested." It is probably best not to go into the particulars or name names and figures. Build a little mystery and competitive spirit, if you are pressed to do so. Try, "I don't think it's appropriate at this stage to give details, but the firm is also a nonprofit and has a competitive compensation range."

- *Get some objective perspective.* Before deciding to take the job, carefully recall the preferred job criteria and career direction you established at the start of your search. And be sure to involve and assess both your reason and feelings in the decision. One way to proceed is to complete the form in Figure 9.1: (For more details on this decision-making process, see Chapter 8, *Hire Me, Inc.*, Entrepreneur Press).

> **HITS** (Hints, Insights, and Thoughts)
>
> Look to see how you made other key decisions in your life. What was your process? Keep this same pattern, if you can, and try to apply both logic and instinct to a series of exercises and activities. Get your left and right brain working together, but remember to *save this energy until after you have your offer letter in hand*. Hold yourself back from what-ifs. Too often people expend effort on situations that never materialize.

Figure 9.1: **Pros and Cons of Position**

Pros

_____

_____

_____

Cons

_____

_____

_____

Other Factors

_____

_____

_____

Other questions you might consider in making your final decision:

- How excited am I about the opportunity? (Like winning a lottery?)
- How does the position lead to my long-term career goals and match my skills, interests, and values?
- How will my work priorities be established? (Is there more than one person I will report to?)
- What are the skill sets of my employees? (Education and range of experience, too?)
- How does the position fit into the overall organization?
- What is the success or failure rate of others who have held the same position?
- What obstacles might prevent me from being successful?
- How does the company deal with its people performance problems?

- Is there a printed and posted mission statement? How is it being fulfilled?
- How would accepting or rejecting the job impact my financial situation?
- Does the total compensation meet or exceed my minimum requirement?
- What are the current opportunities in my job market and the job economy in general?

If you have multiple offers or the position presents a radical career shift or lifestyle change, the strain of making the right decision may continue. If so, here are some additional tips that could help ease that stress:

- Talk over the issues with a confidant, partner, or professional. Sometimes hearing your descriptions of the various opportunities can be telling, and (s)he can pick up your enthusiasm or fears easier than you can.
- Imagine the role. Once you're comfortable with a decision, sleep on it, then daydream the outcome. See if you can imagine yourself in each situation and play it out in your mind, if you can. Very often the right decision will be confirmed for you.

If you decide this is not the best career move and/or the position is not right for you at this time, let your contacts at the organization know as soon as you can. Call and explain your reasons and regret (especially to anyone with whom you connected well). Cite differing personal career needs and long-term goals rather than problems with the organization or its personnel. If you are still interested in the organization, though not the particular job, emphasize your faith in the company and its goals or how you were impressed with the team. Reaffirm that you wish to be considered for other openings that are a better fit. Often an especially effective recruiter, HR talent scout, or hiring manager will remember you and call you again for another opportunity. Besides, you may meet some of the company's people again at an industry function and your last impression with them can leave as much impact as your first.

You are in the driver's seat once you have the offer letter in hand. You have effectively sold yourself and are now in the power position. You are in control. You can head wherever you want to go. No matter how sweet the offer might be, you can negotiate, you should negotiate, and you need not accept the conditions of employment until your short- and long-term career needs are met. Today, most employers expect some negotiation over the job terms. This is not the same as haggling over the price/value of a product, such as a car; it is simply setting proper terms early to establish your stance and leverage in future salary discussions with your management.

Negotiation should not be confrontational, rushed, or completed to only one side's satisfaction. In certain jobs—sales and purchasing, for example—negotiation skills are key to success, and you may still be evaluated on your approach. See the experience as the ultimate win-win engagement for you and the organization by establishing your individual worth and productive value to the organization. Figure 9.2 give some specific negotiables and/or reference points for your analysis.

Figure 9.2: **Analysis Sheet**

❑ Annual bonus plans and sign-up

❑ Annual physical

❑ Base pay

❑ Day care facilities or reimbursement

❑ Deferred compensation

❑ Dependent tuition

❑ Disability

❑ Enhanced insurance packages

❑ Executive protection package (severance/outplacement monies)

❑ Incentives and stock options

❑ Insurances—term life, medical, dental

❑ Keogh

❑ Memberships/dues

❑ Pension, 401K

❑ Performance/salary reviews (time, frame)

❑ Personal professional development

❑ Professional conference costs

❑ Relocation costs—present and future

Figure 9.2: **Analysis Sheet,** continued

❏   Sales commissions

❏   Scope of responsibility

❏   Spouse outplacement

❏   Staff professional development

❏   Start date

❏   Travel upgrade

❏   Tuition reimbursement

❏   Use of company facilities

❏   Vacation, sick days, sabbaticals

HITS (Hints, Insights, and Thoughts)

Remember everything is negotiable. Most employers expect a counter and factor in for a discussion. Pick something to negotiate—perhaps an item that has a certain amount of flexibility or no direct out-of-pocket expense. Asking is always OK. No need to be sensitive about it. How you ask and how you deal with the answer is worthy of some practice.

The base salary is probably your first point of negotiation. It's important to do some homework before you begin this part of your discussion. If you are new to the work force or if you are starting a new career, you might want to talk to a professional in the field to check for typical salary ranges for your position and to gather some baseline figures. You can also look to salary guides or the internet (such as www.salary.com) to pinpoint appropriate ranges. If you are changing jobs, you may know a current salary range for your role in the industry and have a fair, set market value in mind.

Here are some tips that might help in your negotiations:

• Talk to industry professionals about their views on your salary range and compensation guidelines.

• Scan ranges listed in classified advertisements for similar openings.

Chapter 9: Close Down and Next Steps

- Call recruiters or industry associates and inquire about typical base salary ranges.
- Visit the library for additional reference materials listing job titles and pay scales, with recent wage and salary surveys, for example.
- Search the internet for sites that provide the data (see Chapter 6).
- Remember, several factors influence the salary range—the job's location, company size, other benefits provided—so you should not restrict your figure to simple dollar-for-dollar comparisons.
- Note some key economic realities:
  - The cost of labor cannot be precisely determined.
  - The level of compensation rises with the level of contribution and responsibility.
  - The employee exists to make a profit for the organization.
- Be sure you understand the company's perspective and the information it has at hand, including:
  - How much you were earning at your previous position.
  - How long the search has been ongoing and how difficult it has been to find the ideal candidate.
  - How long you have been on the market.
  - How many other candidates are suitable and available.
  - How much financial flexibility the company has. Larger organizations, with strictly defined and well-researched ranges and honored corporate compensation philosophies are often bound by precedence and have internal equity issues as well. They instruct their managers to bring new hires into the lower part of a three-part range. Smaller, less-structured firms might have more room to work with candidates on a case-by-case basis.

The negotiation is a balancing act. Again, your goal is to create a win-win situation where you and the organization both benefit and each is satisfied. If you choose to accept the job, begin the new association on a positive note. Be sure to begin enthusiastically. Try saying: "I'm really very interested in pursuing this opportunity and am eager to talk about a few issues." "I'm really excited about the offer, though I do want to talk about a few issues or particulars that need some clarification." "I'm looking forward to getting started, and your offer is a solid one, but I do have a few concerns we need to talk about."

When discussing salary, you ought to counter with a question: "How have you ranged this position?" "Where is this figure in the range?" "How much movement is there in this figure?" Keep your tone upbeat and positive. But as a matter of course, ask for 10 to 15 percent more than the minimum salary you will accept. Everything may be adjusted, not just base pay; you can negotiate bonus, relocation, stock options, etc. Once a figure is identified, it is unlikely to increase beyond this discussion stage. Make sure your stock reflects a percentage in the company rather than a set number of shares, and that you can secure a change of control clause, a severance package, or executive protection plan as additional protection.

Ask for a sign-on bonus and all of the perks that come with this title or organizational level. You don't want to learn on your first week of work that every other Senior VP has a Country Club membership, but you don't.

Present your requirements in ranges, and organize your target salary into various increments. For example, $75,000 per year reduces to $6,250 per month or $1,562.50 per week. These figures will help you plot the financial means to meet your expenses, savings, and entertainment funding.

Be prepared to justify your base salary request, perhaps citing your industry research and using words such as "value," "contribution," "value-added," "ability" to succeed, or "experience" to apply skills immediately. Avoid offering reasons like your huge debts or extensive living expenses. Express any disappointment in the salary offer by citing other expectations, saying: "Well, my expectations were in the _____ range." "My professional need is for a higher base."

Remember to apply the assumptive sales technique, and use "we," "our company," and "our goals" to reinforce your commitment and eagerness to work for the organization.

If you are unsuccessful in gaining your preferred compensation, you can ask for an early compensation discussion/review, perhaps in about the first four to six months on the job. Be careful, however, as a mere performance review may not include the incentive of a raise.

Remember to judge how the total compensation impacts your long-term career goals. Even if you are unsuccessful in any of your negotiated items, you have not lost anything by asking.

Below are some frequently asked questions and answers that can also help:

Q: What if the first figure presented is more than I wanted? Should I still negotiate for more?

A: Maybe. Accept the figure, but don't underestimate your market value and be sure the amount is in the top of your expected scale. Let your data guide you here.

Q: What can I do if the organization refuses to increase the base salary?

A: Be as creative as you can. See if you can expand the role's responsibilities and influence to gain an upgraded job description. Or obtain a sign-on bonus, commission plan, or an early compensation review.

Q: How much leverage can I use by mentioning that I have another offer?

A: You can mention that other organizations are interested, but be careful. Make it clear that your preference is this package and organization, and you hope a compromise is available. If you are overassertive or demanding, you could disqualify yourself.

Q: What is my option if the compensation offer is firm and significantly less than I was making before?

A: It depends. Consider what the position offers you long term and what you can learn from the experience. Perhaps the role can provide a positive change of work environment for you, including a more supportive boss or growth-oriented team. If you are promised other benefits in lieu of a higher base pay, make sure these are explained in writing in the event the person giving you his verbal assurance later leaves the organization.

Q: How can I say "no" to the salary presented without nixing the offer?

A: Establish your genuine interest in the position and your commitment and confidence to bring value by saying, "I'm still unsettled with the base pay. Can we structure this for our mutual

> **HITS** (Hints, Insights, and Thoughts)
>
> If at all possible, try to arrange for your partner or spouse to join you on the look-at-the-new-location-area expedition. Some companies will pay for someone to join you. Use your own resources if that does not happen. Moving is a tough transition and making decisions without your partner is too risky.

satisfaction? I'm determined to work with you and make the job reward-ing for both of us."

Q: If I'm working with a recruiter or search firm, who should do the nego-tiation?

A: It is the responsibility of the recruiter to convey your requirements for the position. If everything is in place, then she did a fine job. If the proposal package is less than you expected, it is OK to request a meeting to final-ize the negotiations and to let your contact know you are not completely satisfied.

Q: Should I apologize for any difficulty in the negotiation?

A: Not at all. You shouldn't regret trying to get the best or most appropri-ate salary for your services. In fact, you can emphasize that this is how you do business in driving a hard bargain with clients, customers, and vendors to get the best value for the organization.

Q: If my start date is sooner than I expect, can I extend it?

A: Let your contact know when you planned to begin work. Explain that you have set vacation plans, family commitments, or key projects to com-plete before leaving your present organization. Mention your standards of excellence and desire to honor all involved in this transition.

Q: How is the agreement finalized?

A: When the offer letter is revised to your satisfaction and signed by you and the organization.

Sometimes relocation is involved in accepting a new job. This may require a special negotiation. You may ask for a lump sum to cover moving costs you have researched and arranged. Share any relevant expense documents and esti-mates from your moving company, storage facility, and/or temporary housing rental. Some firms prefer to assign a relocation firm to work with you. Try establishing the following details:

- Who will pay for your trips to look for a new home? Will the same expenses be covered for your spouse or partner as well?

- Who will pay for you to commute to the job or pay for temporary hous-ing until you get settled?

- Who will cover any losses in selling your present home?
- Who will cover taxes, interest—even utilities—on your present home until it sells?
- Who will pay for points and closing costs or provide additional help with a down payment or special loan?
- Who will pay for outplacement or career counseling for your spouse or partner?
- Who will arrange for renting or leasing your present home if it doesn't sell quickly?
- Who will pay for the boats and cars to be shipped?

Though employment contracts are used less frequently in today's job market, you may want to retain an attorney to oversee the terms. Make sure the terms are clear on the bonus plan, termination clause, and proprietary information requirements before you sign. These three criteria are typically the most crucial in finalizing a contract.

ALERTING/THANKING YOUR NETWORK

Once you have successfully negotiated the terms of your new position, signed your offer letter, and confirmed a start date, you can close your job search. Remember to inform contacts at prospect companies, hiring managers you've met, recruiters and other job search professionals, your family, friends/colleagues—your entire network if possible—that you have landed a new job. Send them your thanks, and a new business card, as soon as you have a direct phone line and corporate e-mail. See Figure 9.3 for three examples of contact thank-yous.

Another good news announcement to create is the internal one that will introduce you to your new organization. If at all possible, work with your new boss to craft this letter. You want to be sure your arrival is positioned in the most positive way possible. Provide background information and a

> **HITS** (Hints, Insights, and Thoughts)
>
> Too many things can happen between when you get your offer and when you sit at your desk on that first day of work. Hold back your thank-you and good news announcement until you are on the job and settled in. It can be embarrassing to have to contact everyone and let them know the position fell through last minute.

Figure 9.3: **Sample Contact Thank-You Letter**

Example 1

Date: July 15, 200X
From: Lucky Lu
To: Harry Simmons
Subject: Good News

Dear friends and colleagues,

I'm pleased and excited to inform you that I have joined PAS—the world's largest supplier of computer software—as an Organization Development Manager as of June 4.

I will be working on management skill training and a new manager survival/orientation guide, and as a faculty presenter at PAS University. As you know, these are all tasks I enjoy, and I'm looking forward to making a significant contribution.

I want to thank everyone who helped in my career transition, and I hope to stay in touch through our thriving network.

My new work contact information:
    E-mail: Lu@PASinternational.com
    Phone: (610) 661-3096
    Fax: (610) 661-3097

Thanks again,

Lucky Lu

Example 2

From: Sonny Day
Sent: Monday, August 27, 200X
To: List
Subject: New Position at Metrinet

Dear friends,

Here's some good news! I joined Metrinet as Vice President of Information Technology in mid-August to help transition wireless internet service into reality for the next decade. Metrinet provides data communication from Los Feliz, CA. In my new role, I will work to optimize the current system design and initiate new plans for higher speed applications. I'm looking forward to the challenge.

Figure 9.3: **Sample Contact Thank-You Letter,** continued

I want to thank you and the many people who have supported me during my job search and to give everyone my new contact information.

I can be reached by phone at (408) 399-8410 and via e-mail at sonnyd@metrinet.com. I look forward to keeping in touch with each of you.

Best wishes,

Sonny Day
Vice President, Information technology
Metrinet, Inc.

Example 3

From: Jill Job-Satisfac
Sent: Monday, September 16, 200X
To: List
Subject: CareerMate's New Marketing Manager

Family and friends:

Thank you. Thank you.

Effective September 3, I joined CareerMate in San Francisco as its new Marketing Manager. CareerMate, for those who might not know, is a start-up organization that provides both individual and group career development services, and I will be responsible for introducing the company's offerings to the marketplace.

I also hope to do some direct service seminar delivery and one-on-one counseling. This is the ideal job for me right now, and I am thrilled at the opportunity.

I would not have obtained this role without your support and encouragement, and I am most appreciative.

Feel free to contact me, and know that I will do whatever I can to stay in touch and help you however you'd like.

My best,

Jill Job-Satisfac
Marketing Manager
CareerMate, Inc.
Phone and Fax (415) 637-3000
E-mail: JJobsatis@CareerMate.net

photo, but make sure you can get approval before the letter is distributed. This is another marketing tool and can often set the tone for your acceptance, credibility, and future success.

For example, a Ph.D. researcher took her first industry position as a member of the staff of a training and development organization committed to validating the effectiveness of its programs. Her announcement highlighted her thesis topic—"Study of Inter-Cultural Aspects of the Sri Lankan Fourth Generation and Its Impact on the 3–6 Grade School Curricula"—which did nothing to establish her credibility as a business professional who would be interacting with peers to validate key behavior changes from training. For years this presentation was a laughingstock throughout the organization. Take care that your first steps or reports are relevant to your new organization's business.

STARTING FRESH: THE FIRST 90 DAYS

This information on gaining early wins and developing internal networks is excerpted by permission from *Find the Bathrooms First*, Roy Blitzer and Jacquie Reynolds-Rush, Crisp Publications, 1999.

Starting a new job is like many new experiences—fun and scary at the same time. Perhaps it's been awhile since you worked or you are just initially uncomfortable or uneasy in new situations. Here is a chance to test your mettle and an opportunity to begin fresh.

Entering a new organization and mastering a new position is a process that takes time. For a great start—with your boss, staff, internal and external customers, etc.—you need to observe (and ask), learn, and reflect on how the organization operates.

It's difficult to predict and/or control what will happen on the first few days at your new organization, but there are some steps you can take to make the experience much easier. Consider the best- and worst-case scenarios and be ready for either.

Prepare

Create a plan that will give you a good start on the first day. Get a good night's sleep. Try to start your day relaxed. Allow some extra time for your morning routine, wear a favorite—and comfortable—outfit or lucky piece of clothing (obviously one that is consistent with the company's culture and dress code), eat what you love most for breakfast, and allow extra commute time to reach your destination. If you have child-related responsibilities, plan for a trusted support system of people to back you up. Call to verify the start time and try to set up a brief meeting with your boss to touch base on the first day.

Bring Some Supplies

Take along a "briefcase" of materials. Along with a calendar and/or your time organizer, include a highlighter, Post-Its,® and notepad paper. Know something about your first project and be ready to begin work on a portion of it. Have a copy of your offer letter and other paperwork with you. Carry your cell phone with you. Sometimes there is no phone at your desk. Sometimes you don't even have a desk. Give the number to the receptionist in case someone internally wants to contact you. Plan in advance to limit/monitor all outside phone contact.

Without such preparation, you could spend your first day bored, out of place, and out of sorts. Your goal is to be a productive addition immediately.

Bring Some Company Literature and Lists

Ask your key contact or the human resource group to forward all pertinent corporate literature, a directory of names and phone numbers, an organization chart, or even some biographical information on key stakeholders in your new network. Carry these documents with you and take advantage of time to read and memorize them.

Bring Your Wits and Wisdom

Sometimes on your first day you're immediately swept into the eye of the storm. Long overdue work has been left for you, an emergency has arisen, or a meeting has been organized that involves your input. Sometimes your first day has been so overplanned that you can't catch your breath. Do what needs to be done, but go easy on giving advice. Give yourself more time to understand the situation; it's OK to be clear that you're new and want to learn more about the company before making suggestions. This is especially challenging for the forceful personality or for someone who needs to be in the limelight immediately. Be a good listener. It's hard to learn much by talking all the time.

Take Care of Yourself

Bring something that will brighten up your work space—a family photo, a candy dish, a ceramic pencil holder, or a desk set. It's important that your space be comfortable and feels like it's yours. Your office personalization sends a message about who you are to your co-workers. Be flexible about plans for lunch, so you can take care of whatever opportunities may come up. Have a good friend or someone who works nearby as your backup. Be prepared to stay way beyond the normal workday schedule. Make sure your first evening is as hassle-free as possible. Clear your calendar from all commitments. Maybe crash at the TV or go to a movie. Be sure you unwind and relax.

Indeed, the first day is a monumental one. Anything you can do to build your confidence and demonstrate your commitment to the organization will help. You can begin to take charge, do your best from the "get-go," and make each day count.

Certainly, your first few days and months on the job are critical. Be sure you continue to evaluate your situation and how you are doing. Check some additional tips below that could enhance your success once you are settled in to your new position and in to your groove! Remember, also, that even in a new position you need to be resilient and resourceful, always planning for the future.

- Gather data about your position.
- Make sure you have a formal copy of your job description, if one exists. Create one of your own, if there isn't one, and pick two or three aspects that are likely to give you the most satisfaction and build on them, when creating your goals.
- If the job differs greatly from what you expected, talk with your boss and get clarification. Check with him/her to fully understand the key short- and long-term objectives and how your success will be measured. Set up a means for reporting on your progress, as well. (In a discussion with your boss, ask why you were selected for the position, so you can showcase these skills from the start.)

- Get to know the people. Meet as many internal and external customers as you can and everyone in your work group. Ask how you can be most helpful in working with them and demonstrate you are a team player by listening attentively and ensuring you will keep sensitive information confidential.

- Receive negative information about individuals or the organization with an open mind. Remember not to ignore or embrace this knowledge but to check periodically to see how it matches your perspective during the next few weeks or months. Stay upbeat and responsive and begin to build your relationships on trust and support and help each other succeed. (Avoid forming set opinions of people—good or bad—until you've had time to see them in several work scenarios.)

- Increase your understanding of the organization.

- Review all the literature you read in your preparation phase and meet with someone in public or community relations to better understand the company image.

- Learn as much as you can about both the formal and informal reporting relationships (organization charts), key policies and procedures, influencers, de-facto leaders, grapevine sources, and other relevant aspects of the system. Take notes and observe activities, but maintain an open mind. Remember to keep your observations and opinions to yourself for now and resist joining in any negative banter. You can begin to tackle the genuine problems once you've established your credibility and influence.

- List your accomplishments. Keep track of what you do and how you do it. There should be no surprises at review time.

- Maintain your skills. Look for ways to stay current and to learn more. (Volunteering for certain assignments can always help.)

- Master the change. Take what you've seen that worked and try to apply it

> **HITS** (Hints, Insights, and Thoughts)
>
> Remember to test your reactions to your new position and environment every month for at least a quarter. Ask yourself how the situation compares to your expectations. How are you doing toward achieving your goals or how are your relationships with your boss, key stakeholders, and customers? This kind of assessment will help you monitor your progress and nip any problems in the bud before they become significant or de-motivating.

in your new setting. Reflect on what you have learned about yourself and how to continue to improve your value add.

- Establish firm relationships and continue to build and nurture existing bonds regularly (plan lunches, attend meetings, etc.).

Career Maintenance: Promoting Yourself to the Next Level

Even though you are now in a new position, it's important to acknowledge that you are still selling and promoting yourself. Here are some guidelines to maintain a growing career profile.

- Continue the self-assessment process and seek experiences (management training, professional seminars, etc.) that will help define and strengthen your skills, interests, and values.
- Take an internship or join a cross functional/problem-solving team for exposure to other organizational groups and to master new training. Associate with others in a fast-track career group.
- Continue internet research into your career area and take a few more calculated advancement risks in a positive, flexible way.
- Plan for more organizational or economic change—save money for some financial security in case of another layoff (strive to set up six months' living expenses), invest your resources carefully, and work to stay debt-free.
- Engage a mentor to advise you on your future plans and guide you in maintaining active career enhancements.

The Search Continues

Once you're employed again, you should always keep an eye out for an even better job that may appear. You are still in charge of your work life and professional future. These tips should help you remain alert to new career options:

- Remain aware of the local job market and where your industry is heading.
- Stay connected with your network by meeting regularly with others in your industry.
- Stay current in your field. Read professional journals, take classes, attend development seminars, etc.

- Grow in your current position and find ways to add value to your team and organization, building new success stories.
- Stay in touch with your helpful recruiters—listen to any new jobs they might suggest for you and share names to help them in job searches outside your field. (Keep your resume current at all times as well.)
- Stay focused on your goals and set one-, two- and five-year career development plans that might require additional education degrees, more training, volunteering, etc.
- From now on you will always be ready to move forward, either internally or externally.

CONCLUSION: THE BEST IS ALL YOU CAN GIVE

The interview and its results can be especially rewarding. Have fun with the process. If you applied all of the information and input from the text, there is still no guarantee, unfortunately, that you will get the result you want. Nevertheless, with experimentation and practice you will be successful. Do the best you can with what you have. Things happen for a purpose, and you will benefit in many ways from the preparation and experience of interviewing. Best of good luck.

PTOS (Practical Tips and Opinions)

- Keep your search active until your first day on the new job. Some organizations are not as honorable as they should be and may withdraw an offer as late as the first day of work. Protect yourself and keep your program going until you walk into work and begin your new assignment.

- To help with especially tough job decisions, share your choices with those closest to you by describing the pros and cons of job A and job B. Which description sounds more convincing and comfortable to you?

- Remember to conduct your negotiations—either on the phone or preferably in person—with tact, confidence, and professionalism, as your approach will ease your

PTOS (Practical Tips and Opinions)

entry into the organization and characterize your future job behavior. Good business people negotiate; great business people negotiate well.

- It is most important to understand at the outset that you are worth what the market is willing to pay. The issue is not how much you want or need or were paid before but what your new position is worth and how much you can contribute. Be mindful that your base pay can impact how much money you make long term, as well, because it is the basis for yearly compensation adjustments, bonuses, etc.

- Be sure you know why you were selected for the position so you can validate that good judgment with matching behaviors.

- Statistics show that the average new job is landed after a search that lasts between 16 and 18 months! Remember not to get complacent.

✳ *Summary* ✳

✳ Negotiating is expected and can be fun. Hold back until you get your offer in writing and try to have a face-to-face meeting with the person in charge.

✳ Telegraphing your good news and thanking your constituents is a must-do and will bring positive closure to this portion of your search.

✳ Integrating into your new job—especially your first three months—requires especially good listening and periodically assessing your progress toward expectations will prevent issues from escalating later on.

✳ Managing your career does not end when you land the job of your dreams. Staying professionally current and nurturing your network are activities that need to be constant and ongoing.

INDEX